ACCOUNTING:

HITS.on the Web

PART I

World Wide Web Overview

by

Carol Lea Clark

University of Texas, El Paso

URLs prepared by

Gemmy Allen

North Lake College of the
Dallas County Community College District

THOMSON
CUSTOM PUBLISHING

Editor: **Bob Lamana**
Production / Manufacturing Supervisor: **Donna M. Brown**
Project Coordinator: **Brain Schaefer**
Marketing Manager: **Sara Hinckley**
Electronic Publishing: **Mike Leichman**

Printed in the United States of America

Thomson Custom Publishing
5191 Natorp Blvd.
Mason, Ohio 45040
USA

For information about our products, contact us:
1-800-355-9983
http://www.thomsoncustom.com

International Headquarters
Thomson Learning
International Division
290 Harbor Drive, 2nd Floor
Stamford, CT 06902-7477
USA

UK/Europe/Middle East/South Africa
Thomson Learning
Berkshire House
168-173 High Holborn
London WCIV 7AA

Asia
Thomson Learning
60 Albert Street, #15-01
Albert Complex
Singapore 189969

Canada
Nelson Thomson Learning
1120 Birchmount Road
Toronto, Ontario MIK 5G4
Canada
United Kingdom

Visit us at www.thomsoncustom.com and learn more about this book and other titles published by Thomson Custom Publishing.

ISBN: 0-759-34014-5

The Adaptable Courseware Program consists of products and additions to existing Custom Publishing products that are produced from camera-ready copy. Peer review, class testing, and accuracy are primarily the responsibility of the author(s).

CONTENTS

PART I

WORLD WIDE WEB OVERVIEW

CHAPTER 1

AN INTRODUCTION TO THE WORLD WIDE WEB

The ability to navigate the World Wide Web has become a necessity for college students. Of the five million full-time students in four-year colleges in the U.S, 90% use the Internet daily, according to a *Forbes* article. The percent of students using the Internet in two-year colleges may not be quite as high, but it is increasing rapidly. Many classes have Web pages, and some professors make lecture notes and research materials available only online. Campuses, even dorms, are being wired with fiber-optic cable to make access almost effortless. Students at Drexel University in Philadelphia are at the forefront of what will probably be common in the not too distant future; because of the university's wireless network, they can connect from the dorm's lawn and the gym as well as the library. Colleges and universities that do not have state-of-the-art connections encourage students to find their own Internet connection and may offer suggestions and assistance.

Of course, administrators and professors hope their students are using all this access to work on research for their classes, and that is happening. Knowing your way around the Internet is not just a skill for research in colleges, however. Students also spend hours emailing old friends and making new ones in chat rooms. Some invest their free time playing online games, others play the stock market with their own money. The Internet has become an amazing source of new markets. According to Nielsen/NetRatings and Harris Interactive, online transactions in January 2001 were $3.8 billion. Companies also use the Internet to communicate between offices, as well as a source for research information.

Some criticize the Internet, however, saying that it is slow during peak hours and that finding information is time consuming and frustrating. Others say it is at best a source of frivolous entertainment, and, at worst, a dangerous distraction from classes and homework. These criticisms may all be merited at one time or another, but it is also true that the Internet today is a potentially unlimited store of data, too important to boycott. In addition, efforts are being made on many levels to make the Internet faster by increasing bandwidth and to make information easier to access by refining search methods.

According to Nielsen/NetRatings, in January 2001 Internet access either at home or at work reached 169 million individuals in the United States, 60% of the population. This is an increase of eight percent since October 2000. Global Reach estimates that by 2003, 774 million people worldwide will have Internet access.

The World Wide Web's colorful, graphics-studded, and user-friendly environment appeals to an increasing number of users who may have had neither the patience nor the desire to learn the intricacies of the older and less colorful network protocols that were predominant on the Internet before the Web was developed. (*Protocols* are sets of agreed-on conventions for transferring data across a network.) But the advances of the Web over FTP (file transfer protocol), gopher, and other protocols are more than glitz. The Web offers increased flexibility and a range of media that enhances both the impact and the content of the information transmitted to the user. Indeed, the Web began as a project designed to provide a simple and convenient way to distribute scientific information across computer networks through hypertext. This hypertext interface was fashioned to allow researchers to present their work complete with text, pictures, charts, and illustrations within a system of links that enables the user to move logically from one text section to a related section in much the same way a text note in a book might refer the reader to a related section in another chapter. The hypertext design of the Web quickly matured into a resource with simple controls that anyone can learn to use and master quickly.

Hypertext really isn't new. Print dictionaries and encyclopedias use a rudimentary form of hypertext. The Macintosh HyperCard program and similar programs for Microsoft Windows use hypertext, enabling users to select highlighted items on a computer page and move to linked documents. What is revolutionary about hypertext on the Web, however, is that you can link to a document located on a computer server on your campus and then move with equal ease to documents in Boston or Brazil. Through the World Wide Web, the world has become an interconnected web of hypertext documents.

Is the Web the Internet? No. The Internet (Net) existed long before the Web, and many of the resources on the Internet are still stored in non-hypertext formats for use with older protocols, such as gopher and FTP. The Internet also includes electronic mail (e-mail) and Usenet newsgroups, a collection of some 40,000 discussion groups, which really aren't part of the Web. You can, however, access these non-Web parts of the Internet through a *browser*, a program used to navigate the Web, though they will not be in hypertext.

A Very Brief History of the Internet

The Internet long predates the World Wide Web. It began in the early 1960s as a computer communication network the U.S. military designed to survive a nuclear attack. Because it was decentralized, if one or more portions of the network had been destroyed, the others still could have communicated with each other. The original network was called ARPAnet (Advanced Research Projects Agency). Other networks followed as scientists and researchers discovered the many benefits of communicating with each other. University local area networks and, recently, commercial online services such as America Online and CompuServe have become part of the Internet. The most popular use of the Internet by far has been electronic mail, allowing people to communicate with each other around the world. The World Wide Web, however, with its colorful, user-friendly interface, is attracting millions of new users to the system.

The Internet has no central control. For many years, the acceptable-use policy dictated by the National Science Foundation, a major funding source, restricted the Internet to educational and nonprofit usage. In recent years, however, funding of the Internet has changed and commercial use has grown rapidly.

For a moment, think of what you know about how cable television works. The physical pieces of the Internet can be compared to all the cable and control equipment the cable company provides. The information stored throughout the Internet can be compared to the shows you receive through the cable system. A World Wide Web browser is analogous to the television. It gives you a convenient, easy-to-use interface for all the rich resources on the Internet in much the same way a good television provides you with an easy-to-use interface for viewing your favorite shows. Different television models and brands all provide the same function, though older ones may be in black and white rather than color; similarly, different Web browsers (and different, updated versions of Web browsers) vary in sophistication from text-only to full graphical capabilities. All the browsers, from text-only Lynx to graphical Netscape, access the same information on the World Wide Web. Even cell phones and PDAs with wireless Internet access derive their information from the same Web pages, though the pages have been reformatted to display only parts of their content on the smaller screens.

The Web's Special Characteristics

Until relatively recently, few ventured into cyberspace unless they were die-hard computer enthusiasts, educators, or scientists. The Internet had the appeal of access to huge amounts of information; before the Web, however, the Internet was unadorned and colorless, requiring the use of cryptic command prompts and menus to locate and retrieve information. The Web is a distinct improvement over earlier Internet protocols and interfaces in several important ways:

HYPERTEXT—Key words or points in one document link seamlessly with parts of other documents, whether the documents are stored on the same computer or on separate machines in distant places around the world.

HYPERMEDIA—Web pages look more like slick magazines pages than the text-only offerings of earlier Internet documents. Photos, video, sound, and interactive viewer-to-site communication make many new types of communication possible.

BROWSERS—Programs called browsers display hypertext files and allow the user, with the click of a mouse, to connect to a document and display it. To explore the Web, a user can pick an entry point (such as a university home page) and jump from one site to another, browsing at will. These programs effectively turn cyberspace into what seems like an immense disk drive.

PLUG-IN PROGRAMS—Browsers launch plug-in or auxiliary programs, which display image, sound, and video files. This keeps the size of the browser programs smaller and increases flexibility by enabling browsers quickly to support media as they become available.

ACCESS TO DOCUMENTS IN OTHER FORMATS—The Web also supports connections to documents formatted for transmission via FTP, gopher, WAIS (Wide-Area Information Server), and Usenet newsgroups, making it possible to navigate all of cyberspace without leaving a WWW browser program.

INTERACTIVITY—Many Web documents have built-in interactivity through forms that solicit responses from readers, and many Web documents include connections to Web page authors' e-mail addresses.

SELF-PUBLISHING—For the first time in publishing history, individuals have the capability of publishing documents thousands or even millions may read. All that is required for publishing is a fairly modest knowledge of *HTML* (Hypertext Markup Language) or one of a number of HTML editing programs and access to space on a server (a computer that stores Web documents).

Hypertext Transfer Protocol

Hypertext Transfer Protocol (HTTP) is the backbone of the World Wide Web. It is a series of agreed-on conventions and interlocking programs that

A Very Brief History of the World Wide Web

The Web dates back only to 1990. Based on a proposal by Tim Berner-Lee for enhancing the Internet, CERN (the European Particle Physics Laboratory in Geneva) began work on a hypertext browser. The purpose was to allow researchers to collaborate by presenting research information not only in plain text but also in hypertext with graphics, illustrations, and, eventually, sound and video. By January 1993, fifty Web servers (or computer sites offering files in Web format) existed. That same year the first version of an advanced Web browser called Mosiac was developed by Marc Andreesen at the National Center for Supercomputing Applications (NCSA) in Champaign, Illinois; because of Mosaic's user-friendly interface, interest in the Web began to spread far beyond the scientific community. By 1994, more than ten thousand servers operated, and the Web began to attract media attention, with articles appearing in the *New York Times* and other major newspapers.

make up the Web. Because HTTP is a client-server protocol, you as a user have a *client* program on your computer that uses HTTP to communicate with a remote *server* computer storing information. The remote computer runs the server portion of the Hypertext Transfer Protocol. Every document on the Web has an address (something like http://www.somewhere.edu). When you type in a World Wide Web address or click on a hypertext link, your HTTP client program (also called a browser) attempts to connect to the remote computer you have requested. The address you give your browser also has the name of a file or, by default, the home page file. When a connection to the remote computer is established, the server looks for the file and, if it is found, downloads it to your computer. If the file isn't found, you receive an error message. Once the file downloads from the server, your client program takes over and displays the file according to its format, which may be hypertext, graphics, sound, video, or something else.

Hypertext Markup Language

Hypertext Markup Language (HTML) is a system of codes embedded in text documents that tells a Web client (browser) program how to display the document as hypertext. The codes indicate links to other documents, placement of graphics, headings, alignments, and so on. You don't need to master HTML unless you want to create Web documents yourself. If you simply want to explore the Web and use its resources, your browser program reads and interprets the codes for you.

APPLICATIONS OF THE WORLD WIDE WEB

The Web has become a repository for endless amounts of information on almost any subject imaginable. For example, in Thomas (http://thomas.loc.gov), the site for the United States Congress, you can read or download the full text of pending legislation and check on the status of bills. Because the Web can be updated so quickly, it is also an excellent source for information that changes quickly, such as stock quotes or weather conditions. The chapters that follow in this book explain how to research topics, discuss major research resources, and offer a list of subject-specific Websites in your discipline.

The World Wide Web is a reflection of world culture. It's a quirky and inconsistent mix of serious research, commercial promotion, entertainment, individual opinions, propaganda, and any other type of communication humans can invent. Much out there is valuable; some of it you may consider worthless, and other things may amuse you. Certainly no one person can absorb all the sites; what you can learn are techniques that help you to find what you want to find, whether it be serious research or recreation.

Accessing the World Wide Web via Colleges and Universities

To access the Web, you must have an Internet connection and a browser program, so named because it allows you to browse or explore the Web. If you are a student in a college or university, you may have free or low-cost access to the World Wide Web and the Internet. Likely, you will connect to the Web in one of the following ways:

- ✦ Through computer labs with full graphical browsers such as Internet Explorer or Netscape Navigator installed.
- ✦ By telephone modem access from home provided by your college or university. With this type of connection, you can use Internet Explorer or another graphical browser from your home computer. If your university offers this type of access, it also should provide you with instructions on how to implement it.
- ✦ Computer labs or dial-up modem access with text-only World Wide Web capability. Some universities use Lynx or another text-only browser, which enables you to access the text portions of the World Wide Web but not the graphics, sound, or video. Commonly, Lynx is accessed from a menu-based shell system. Ask at the computer help desk at your university. They can explain how to access the menu either in the university labs or by dial-up remote connection.

Other Options for Access

- Commercial online services such as America Online (AOL) and the Microsoft Network now provide telephone modem connections to the World Wide Web. Most offer free introductory hours to try their services. Then you pay a flat fee per month. These providers may also offer additional services, such as chat rooms (electronic discussions) or research materials that are not part of the Internet.
- Internet service providers, either local or national companies, offer SLIP or PPP full Internet access, including e-mail and other Internet protocols in addition to the World Wide Web. They generally offer no additional services that are not part of the Internet. These providers may also supply you with software and instructions for installation. Their fees may be lower than commercial online services.
- Many cable television companies now offer high-speed modem access via a cable connection. A cable modem is an external devices that connect to a network card installed in your computer. Like other commercial online services, they may offer additional services to their subscribers. An advantage of cable access is that it does not tie up a telephone line while you use the Internet.
- DSL (Digital Subscriber Line) is a relatively new trend in high-speed Internet access. DSL works over existing copper telephone lines and is typically offered by telephone companies. DSL uses a different part of the frequency spectrum than analog voice signals, so it can work in conjunction with your standard analog telephone service, sharing the same pair of wires.

CHAPTER 2

BROWSING THE WEB

The ideal way to browse the World Wide Web is to have the most recent version of a full-graphical browser such as Internet Explorer or Netscape Navigator, running on a fast computer with a fast Internet connection; together these enable you to appreciate all the graphics and sound available on the Web and to explore links with a simple click of the mouse.

Alternatively, an increasing number of users are finding that access to the Internet can be mobile and wireless. Some are using laptop computers with modems. Others, wanting even more portability, are accessing the Web through devices such as Personal Digital Assistants (also called PDAs or handhelds) or cellular telephones.

Some users, however, find they are, at least for the present, restricted to a less-than-optimal connection to the Internet. They may not have access to a full-featured browser, either because of limitations of the computers or of the networks they are using. They are thus restricted to text-only browsers which rarely support any features more advanced than simple text display and links. Still, text-only browsers are available and enable such users to consider important information on the Web.

Internet Explorer and Netscape Navigator are the most popular of the graphical browsers, though specialized browsers still hold their own places on the Net. Internet Explorer and Netscape are used in this book to demonstrate navigating the Web. If you are using another graphics-oriented browser, however, your commands will be similar.

BROWSERS

Client–Server Model

The World Wide Web uses a client-server model. A Web browser is a client program that runs on your computer. When you give instructions to the client program through keystrokes or clicks of a mouse, the client program requests information from a remote computer running a server program. Most obviously, you might instruct that a Web page be downloaded to your computer. A *server* is a computer that stores Web pages, and the *server program* sends the data to your *client* browser program. In general, you need only know how the client part of the client-server model works, and this chapter is about that.

Anatomy of a Web Address

All documents on the World Wide Web have specific addresses called URLs (Universal Resource Locators). A Web address may look something like this:

http://www.mtv.com

Or you may see a variation like **www.mtv.com** without the prefix http://, or even **mtv.com**. These addresses are domain names, or nickname addresses, which are a variation of the organization name and, thus, memorable. Other examples would include http://www.whitehouse.gov, the address for the White House, or http://www.microsoft.com, the address for Microsoft Corporation. Technically, http://www.mtv.com is the correct way to write the Web address for the MTV home page, but recent versions of browsers will also accept **www.mtv.com** or **mtv.com**.

Other Web page addresses may look like this:

http://computer.institution.edu/filename.html

In this URL, the http stands for *hypertext transfer protocol*, a designation that tells the browser program that the document you are requesting is in hypertext format. Next comes the ://, which are simply symbols indicating that an address follows. Next are the name of the computer where the document is housed, a designation of the institution, and the suffix .edu, indicating an educational institution. Other suffixes for Web locations follow:

.com (commercial)

.edu (educational)

.gov (government)

.mil (military)

.net (networking, also used for commercial)

.org (noncommercial)

Addresses also may indicate the country of origin outside the United States. These are, for example,

.jp (Japan)

.uk (United Kingdom)

.nl (The Netherlands)

.ca (Canada)

After the slash mark is the specific document or file name and the .html (or htm) notation, which indicates the file is in *Hypertext Markup Language,* the language used to create hypertext documents.

The Internet Explorer Screen has navigational buttons and pull-down menus across the top and a box at the bottom where Web pages are displayed.

Accessing a Browser Program

If you are using a computer in one of your university's labs, chances are that Internet Explorer or Netscape is installed, and you can launch it by clicking on the browser's icon on your screen or by selecting it from the *Start* button. Your university or college may offer a dial-up connection which allows you to use a browser installed on your computer at home. Many colleges and universities, however, expect students to find their own Internet connections. If that is the case, consult "Other Options for Access" in Chapter 1.

Accessing Internet Explorer or Netscape will call up the browser window, which consists of several menus above the space where Web pages appear.

Essentials for Using the Browser

To begin navigating the Web using a browser, you need to understand only a few basics:

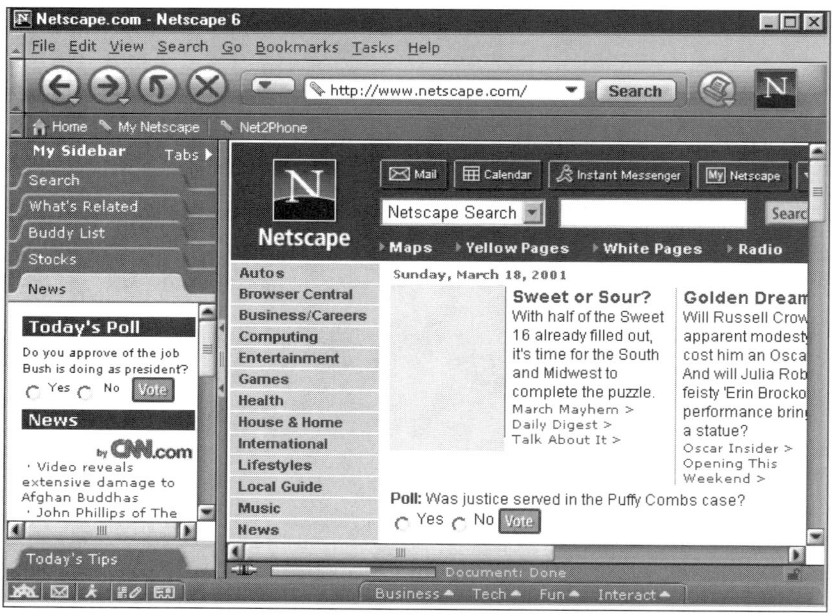

Netscape also offers buttons and pull-down menus for navigating Web pages which appear in the box at the bottom of the screen.

1. From any Web page, you can connect to other Websites by clicking on hypertext links, which are often graphics or photos. Other links may be words that are highlighted and sometimes underlined. It is easy to tell what is a hypertext link (also called a *hot link*), and what is not, by moving the cursor over the word or image. If your cursor turns into a handprint and a Web page address appears at the lower border of the browser, that word or image is a hot link to another page. If you move to a new Web page by clicking on a hypertext link, you can return to your previous page by clicking the *Back* button. You also can move forward to a previously viewed page by clicking on the *Forward* button. Thus, you can navigate throughout the Web by using these two buttons, *Back* and *Forward.*
2. If you know a World Wide Web address and want to connect directly to it, you can do so with either Internet Explorer or Netscape in two ways:
   - ✦ Select *Open* or *Open page* from the *File* pull-down menu, and a dialog box will open. You then can enter the address. Click on *Open* or *Okay* (depending on the browser) in the dialog box, and the browser will connect you to the page represented by that address.
   - ✦ Use the *Address* window near the top of the browser screen to connect to a Web address. Simply highlight the address in the box, begin to type in the desired address (this will delete the previous address), and touch *Enter.* In Internet Explorer, if you don't know the complete address, type part of the address or name of a site, type it into the Address bar, and you'll get a list of possible sites similar to what you typed.
3. A Web page can be of any length, though most are longer than what can be displayed in the box on the computer screen. Use the scroll bar at the right side of the screen to move up and down in a page.
4. Watch the icon in the upper right corner of the browser screen. If the logo is animated, then a transfer is in progress. Note the progress bar at the lower left corner of the page. As a page loads, numbers appear here that show the percentage of the page already downloaded. If the logo is not animated, then your connection is stalled.
5. If you are connecting to a site and it is taking a long time to connect, you may have tried to connect to a location experiencing technical problems. Click on the *Stop* button to abort the attempted connection. Then you can try the connection again or try a different address.

Major Browser Options

PRINT — Click on the Print button or use the *File* menu and select Print.

SAVE	Under the *File* menu, select *Save as*, and you can save the current Web page on a disk or on your hard drive. You have the option of saving as either a text file or an HTML file.
SEARCH	Chick on the *Search* button to receive a page of links to Web search engines. You can enter a key word in one of the search engines, and it will return a list of sites that relate to that topic.
HISTORY	Click the *History* button in Internet Explorer, and you will see a list of sites you have visited recently. Netscape has a similar function, but it is under the *Go* menu at the top of the screen.

NAVIGATING WITH INTERNET EXPLORER

Internet Explorer is loaded ready-to-use in most new PC computers. Each succeeding version of Internet Explorer has new features. For example, Internet

INTERNET EXPLORER'S TOOLBAR BUTTONS

Across the top of the Internet Explorer screen is a series of toolbar buttons that activate features you will use frequently in Internet Explorer.

These are their functions:

Back	Takes you back a page.
Forward	Takes you forward to a previously viewed page.
Stop	Stops the loading of a Web page.
Refresh	Reloads the current page.
Home	Takes you to the default home page for Explorer or to one you have selected.
Search	Links to a search page displaying Web search engines. Internet Explorer 5.5 allows you to specify what type of search you want to do, and Internet Explorer will choose a search service for that type of request.
Favorites	Connects to your list of favorite Websites.
History	Displays a list of Websites you viewed recently. By default, the History bar organizes Web pages in folders by week, then by day. You can choose other options, however. You can, for example, view the history list by pages you visit most often or arranged in alphabetical order.
Mail	Accesses Explorer's mail program.
Print	Prints the Web page.

Explorer 5.5 has an AutoComplete feature. It allows you to type a partial Web address in the Address bar, and a list of potential matches appears. If you've accessed that Web address before, you can simply click on the match and not have to type in the complete address. Another improvement you may find useful in Internet Explorer 5.5 is the ability to preview Web pages exactly as they will appear when printed.

You can download the most recent version from Internet Explorer's home page, http://www.microsoft.com/windows/ie. Version 5.5 requires 486DX/66 MHz or higher processor and Windows 95, Windows 98, or Windows NT 4.0. For Windows 95 and Windows 98, it requires a minimum of 16 MB (megabytes) of RAM, and for Windows NT it requires a minimum of 32 MB of RAM.

The purposes of Internet Explorer's primary buttons and menus are outlined in the following boxes, and Internet Explorer also offers help screens that have additional documentation.

Navigating with Netscape

Netscape is a preferred choice for some users. If your computer is a fairly new one, it came with Internet Explorer already installed. If you decide to

Internet Explorer's Primary Menus

Across the top of the screen above the buttons is a series of pull-down menus that enable you to take advantage of many of Internet Explorer's features.

Briefly, the menus have these and other functions:

File Offers connection to many of the main browser functions, some of which also have buttons, such as *open* (for opening the Website), *save* (to save a Web page), *print*, and *close*

Edit Allows you to save all or a portion of the text content of a Web page

View Enables you to control the tools visible on your browser screen (such as the standard buttons and address box) and also to open a box that displays the HTML content of the current page

Favorites Provides a connection to a list of Websites you designate as favorites; this feature may not be usable in a computer lab

Tools Use to access mail and newsgroups

Help Connects you to Explorer's many help screens

use Netscape Navigator, part of Netscape Communicator, you can download the latest version from the Netscape site, http://www.netscape.com. Explore the pull-down menus and buttons at the top of the Netscape page. The purpose of each is outlined in the following boxes, and Netscape itself offers documentation in help screens that can be assessed from the *Help* pull-down menu.

PLUG-INS AND WEB ACCESSORIES

Plug-ins are software programs, often created by other software companies, that run as auxiliaries to a Web browser and expand its capabilities. Real Audio, for example, is a plug-in that allows the computer to play sound files as they are downloaded to your computer.

You should have Netscape Navigator 2.0 or later, or Internet Explorer 3.0 or later, to install plug-ins. Recent versions of the browsers offer some plug-ins as part of normal installation. Internet Explorer now includes Macromedia Flash and Macromedia Shockwave Player as part of standard installation.

When you access a site, if your computer does not have the correct plug-in, a box will pop up offering you a link to a site where you can download the plug-in. Connect to the plug-in's download site, and download it just as you would any other program. If you are in a lab, the computer likely has settings that will not allow you to download additional plug-ins. If so, check with the lab assistant about how to proceed; a designated computer might have the plug-in, or the staff may be able to add it for you.

Using a plug-in is easy. Some are activated simply by accessing a Web page that requires it. With others, like RealAudio, you click on a hot link to activate the plug-in.

Web Accessories are also utilities, but their function is to allow you to customize Internet Explorer by adding toolbar buttons or Explorer bars that stay open in the browser while you surf to different Websites. For example, you can have explorer bars which provide current stock quotes or breaking news stories. If you are interested, check out the Web Accessories page which can be accessed from the Internet Explorer home page.

FAVORITES OR BOOKMARKS

One of the most useful customized features of Web browsers is the Favorites or Bookmark option, which allows you to save the names and URLs of sites on the Net you would like to access easily. In Internet Explorer, you can add a bookmark to a Web page you are viewing by going to the *Favorites* pull-down menu and selecting *Add to Favorites*. In Netscape, click the Bookmarks icon and select *Add to Bookmarks*.

NETSCAPE'S TOOLBAR MENUS

Across the top of the Netscape screen is a series of toolbar buttons that activate features you will use frequently in Netscape.

These are their functions:

Left arrow Back to the previous page
Right arrow Goes forward to the next page
Curved arrow Reloads the current page
Letter X Stops loading of the page
Search Connects to Netscape's search page
Print Prints document

NETSCAPE'S PRIMARY MENUS

Across the top of the screen above the buttons are a series of pull-down menus that enable you to take advantage of many of Netscape's features.

Briefly, the menus have these and other functions:

File Accesses many features such as Open Web Page and Save Page As (save to a file on your computer).
Edit Allows you to Copy (puts a copy of highlighted text on the clipboard), Select All (highlights everything on the current page so you can copy), and Find (finds a word in the current page).
View Reloads the page, shows the Page Source (displays HTML codes as well as text), and provides Page Info (title, location, date of last modification).
Search Connects to the Netscape Search page.
Go Reviews a list of the sites you have visited in your session, which is useful if you decide you want to reexamine a site.
Bookmarks Connects to list of sites you have marked as favorites.
Tasks Connects to Mail and Instant Messenger.
Help Connects to Netscape's Help screens

VIEWING PAGES OFFLINE

Internet Explorer 5.5 allows to you save pages for viewing offline which can be useful if you are not connected to the Internet at all times. You simply save a Web page to your Favorites list as usual but also check the box that specifies making the item available offline. You can also update all your favorite pages at the same time by using the *Synchronize* command on the *Tools* menu.

DEFAULT HOME PAGE

When you open a browser program, it immediately accesses a particular page. If you would like, for example, to have your browser set to connect to the *New York Times* home page, you can do so. To change to a different home page in Internet Explorer, go to the page you want, click the **Tools** menu, and then click **Internet Options**. On the **General** tab, click **Use Current**. In Netscape, go the *Edit* menu and select *Preferences*. You can then indicate your preference for a default home page.

OTHER PROTOCOLS

Some documents on the Internet are not in hypertext format. Sometimes you will find that a link from a Web page will take you to a gopher or FTP document. These documents will look different from Web documents because they do not have color or graphics. Also, you can identify them because the address displayed once you connect to them will not be a Web address. FTP and gopher sites are organized by directories or menus rather than hypertext links.

If you are using a library online catalog or connect to an interactive online text game such as a MUD or MOO, your browser may use a Telnet client to connect you to the remote computer. Telnet site commands vary, but usually a help file will instruct you on the basic commands of each site.

You may have a specific address of a document not in HTML format. You can access these through the Web by using an address designation, specifying the type of document followed by the address. These are the main file type designations:

gopher://address	telnet://address
ftp://address	news://address

Personal Digital Assistants (PDAs or Handhelds) and Cellular Telephones

At time of publication, surfing the Web with a handheld or cellular telephone may be the ultimate in Web portability, but it is vastly different than the full-graphical Web interface you have probably come to expect. What you see on a handheld or cell phone screen are Web "clippings" that are condensed text-only versions of certain Web pages that have agreed to accommodate the handheld and/or cellular telephone format. Yes, you can access stock quotes and other crucial information but certainly not everything on the Web. However, options for access are becoming more extensive all the time, with experiments such as the offering of Stephen King's "Dreamcatcher" in downloadable ebook format for PDAs.

Things to Remember

1. Web browsers such as Internet Explorer and Netscape Navigator, programs used to explore the Web, are fairly user friendly. Once you have accessed the program, you can learn its features largely by trial and error, clicking on buttons to see what they do.
2. You can use a Web browser to jump from one page to another by clicking on the hypertext links, or you can type in a specific Web address in the *Address* window and then press *Enter*.
3. Internet Explorer and Netscape offer user help. Select the *Help* pull-down menu.

CHAPTER 3

Finding Information on the World Wide Web

The World Wide Web is an incredible resource for research. Through it, you can find full text of pending legislation, searchable online editions of Shakespeare's plays, environmental impact statements, stock quotes, and much, much more.

Finding the research sources you need, however, is not always easy. Research on the Web is far more than surfing. It involves developing a purpose for your research; making a research plan; searching using the different types of access resources, such as subject indexes, keyword search engines, online libraries, and links to magazines. It also involves evaluating the material for relevance, accuracy, and bias.

The Internet is immense, and its research materials are seemingly endless. For example, if you enter the word *environment* in one of the keyword search engines, you may receive thousands of "hits," or sites that relate to that topic from all over the world. How do you sift through all of that feedback in order to find information germane to your topic? It is a problem that hasn't been completely solved on the Internet. However, some strategies will help.

Managing Information

Define Your Purpose

As with any library research project, you need to begin by analyzing your research problem. If you are doing research for a class, your instructor may have given you the assignment in writing. Read it closely. What does your instructor ask you to do? Does he or she ask you to describe something such as environmental resources on the Internet or current treatments for AIDS patients? If so, you will be writing an *informative paper*. You will need to research the topic closely and then to summarize information related to that topic for your audience. An informative paper is more than a summary, however. You will need to focus the information in an original way that illuminates the subject for your audience.

Your assignment may ask you to argue a position or to persuade your audience to behave in a certain way. For example, you may be asked to argue for or against current practices in environmental protection. If so, you will be writing an *argumentative paper*. You will need to research your topic until you can develop a position about your topic and support that position with evidence.

Make a Research Plan

Will you be using the Internet simply as one research tool along with print texts and CD-ROM databases? For many topics, some of the most current information can be found on the Web, and it can greatly enhance your information collection. Or will you be gathering all your information from the Internet? Not all topics have equal coverage on the Internet, but for many subjects (if your instructor agrees) you can collect everything you need without leaving your computer terminal. This chapter discusses the following types of resources for locating research information on the Web.

SEARCH ENGINES—Sites that allow you to search with one or more keywords for your subject or to explore sites by topic indexes. Most search engines also have subject indexes that allow you to follow branching topical menus.

MEDIA LINKS—Sites that allow you to find full-text magazine and newspaper articles on your subject.

FULL-TEXT LIBRARY DATABASES—Your college library may offer Web access to full-text databases of magazine, journal, and newspaper articles.

LIBRARIANS' SUBJECT INDEXES—Indexes to the Web organized by topic with Websites that librarians select

When making a research plan, you need to consider your assignment. Does it say, "Write an argumentative essay about an environmental problem such as toxic waste or acid rain"? If so, you know you need to narrow the topic from the environment in general to a more specific topic such as toxic waste and perhaps to an even more specific topic such as programs for nuclear waste disposal or the recycling of environmentally damaging substances. If you aren't sure what specific topic interests you, you will need to look first at some general sources about the environment to help you choose a topic.

Several research resources on the Web can help you narrow a topic and then gather information about it.

You might, for example, examine some of the online magazines that deal with environmental topics, or you might examine the subject indexes, which might have a heading and subheadings on environmental issues. Subject indexes can be found both in search engine sites and in librarians' subject index sites. How to use these indexes will be discussed later in the chapter. Browsing these resources, you may, for example, narrow your topic to community programs for recycling.

Once you have decided on a narrow topic such as community programs for recycling, you can use the other subject indexes, keyword search engines, full-text databases, and media links to find additional resources. As you locate resources, assemble them in a working bibliography, which will help you keep track of them also as potential resources. Remember that research is a repetitive process. As you explore sources, you may find yourself changing the narrow topic you have selected, and this will require you to find additional sources. Even when you reach the writing stage of your project, you still may need to locate information sources to fill holes in your argument. The research is not complete until the project is complete.

Develop a Working Bibliography

A working bibliography for a World Wide Web research project is a list of sites and their URLs (addresses), as well as articles you may find in online

Sample Working Bibliography

Topic: Violence on Television

Linn, Susan. "Sellouts." *American Prospect.* 23 Oct 2000: 17-20. (Periodical Abstracts database)

Schroeder, Ken. "TV Teaches Violence." *Educational Digest* Sept. 1998: 74-75 (Periodical Abstracts database)

"TV Violence is pervasive..." *National Coalition on TV Violence.* <http:www.nctvv.org>

"Two New Studies on Television Violence and Their Significance for the Kids' TV Debate." The UCLA Television Violence Monitoring Report (September 1995) UCLA Center for Communication Policy and National Violence Study (February,1996) Mediascope, Inc. <http://www.cep.org/tvviolence.html>

"Violence on Television: What do Children Learn? What Can Parents Do?" American Psychological Association. <http://www.apa.org/pubinfo/violence.html>

"When Good Networks Go Bad: Rampaging animals...cheating spouses...big ratings... shockumentaries are hot!" *Time.* 1 Feb. 1999 <http://www.time.com/time/magazine/article/0,9171,19170,00.html>

RESEARCH STRATEGY FOR WORLD WIDE WEB SOURCES

1. Using a subject index (either in a search engine or a librarians' subject index), browse sites in your general topic. See what kinds of information are available on what specific topics.
2. Check online media links for articles on your general topics.
3. Search one or more of your library's full-text periodical databases for your general topic.
4. Narrow your search to a specific enough topic to write about in the length of research paper you intend to prepare.
5. Use one or more keyword search engines to locate relevant sites. Use advanced search options (described later in this section) to customize your search.
6. Compile the resources you have identified into a working bibliography. As you read through the materials available at different sites, continue to explore and record links they offer to related sites.

publications and full-text databases your library provides online. As you browse these resources, you will see many that seem relevant to a possible research project. Write down the URLs or article locations. Otherwise, if you want to return to a particular site or article, you may not remember the sequence that led you to it. The brief working bibliography below was compiled while researching violence on television.

Evaluate Your Sources

Many people tend to believe what they see in print. If information is in a book or a news magazine, it must be true. If you read critically, however, you know that all sources must be evaluated. Does a source give a balanced reporting of the evidence, or does it display bias? What resource sources are cited? What authorities? With the Internet, perhaps even more than with print texts, it is important to evaluate your sources. Undoubtedly, much reliable and valuable information is published through the Web, and you should not hesitate to use sources that, in your judgment, are credible. Remember, though, not all information on the Web is accurate. Anyone with a Web connection and a little knowledge can create a site, and automated search engines will include them in their databases. Also, many sites are commercial and may have their own marketing reasons for promoting certain information. Before relying on information, ask yourself the questions listed in "Evaluating Web Sources" below.

Evaluating Web Sources

1. Who is the sponsoring organization or individual? If no author or sponsoring organization is listed, you have no way to ascertain the document's quality.
2. If an author or sponsor is listed for the site, are any credentials offered that establish credibility? Does anything indicate that the individual/organization has expert knowledge about the topic? Does anything indicate the individual might have bias toward the topic?
3. What are the criteria for including information at the site? Are the documents collected for a stated reason? If so, does that reason enhance or detract from the apparent validity of the information?
4. If it is a business or corporate site, is its purpose marketing or sales? If so, how does that affect any content information at the site?
5. If it is a advocacy page (attempting to influence public opinion), does the organization give you an address or telephone number for verifying their legitimacy? Is it clear that the Web page has the sanction of the official organization?
6. What about the texts? Do they offer a balanced viewpoint? Do they cite sources for the evidence they offer to support their arguments?
7. Is the site technologically sophisticated? Do the graphics or other presentation elements add to or distract from the textual content?

Of course, you may be intentionally studying biased sources on the Web such as home pages of political candidates, special interest groups, or companies selling products. If so, do not take their information at face value. Indeed, you can make your evaluation of biased texts part of your argument. You could, for example, compare what a company selling a health food supplement says about that product with what you read in your search of other texts related to that product (perhaps including scientific studies). One of the Web's revolutionary aspects is that individuals and organizations can put their side of the story directly before the public. It is part of your job as a Web consumer to evaluate critically the motivation or validity of these direct-to-the-public texts.

Search Engines

The Web has a wide variety of searching tools, and more are added as the Web continues to grow. Keyword search engines are the most visible of the

SAMPLE SEARCH

Subject Index

Suppose your instructor has asked you to write an essay about an environmental issue. You don't have a clear idea about a topic and decide to explore. Connect to one of the search engines that has a subject index such as Yahoo! (http://www.yahoo.com). Examine the subject entry on the *Environment and Nature* under *Society and Culture*. You can click on any of the subtopics to receive a list of sites related to that subtopic. Or you can specify a search term in the box given for keywords (be sure also to click on the button that indicates to search only in that subcategory).

After browsing a number of the categories under environment and nature in Yahoo! (or another of the subject indexes), you may be able to narrow your topic, perhaps to recycling and then, even more specifically, to community programs for recycling.

Before you decide on a topic for your paper, however, you may want to peruse what other subject indexes have to offer because each is different. When you have a firm topic, you can try a keyword search.

YAHOO!

Categories

- Business *(13)*
- Climate Change *(58)* NEW!
- Companies@
- Conservation *(274)*
- Disasters *(151)*
- Ecology@
- Ecotourism@
- Education *(141)*
- Employment *(27)*
- Energy@
- Environment and Development Policies *(16)*
- Environmental Economics *(21)*
- Environmental Health@
- Environmental Justice *(22)*
- Environmental Psychology@
- Environmental Security *(9)*
- Environmental Studies *(79)* NEW!
- Environmentalists *(70)*
- Institutes *(81)*
- Legal Issues@
- Meteorology@
- Mining Issues@
- Mountains *(139)*
- Natural History Museums *(85)*
- Nature Centers *(296)* NEW!
- Nature Writing@
- News and Media *(161)*
- Oil and Gas Issues@
- Organizations *(3421)* NEW!
- Overpopulation@
- Ozone Depletion *(22)*
- Parks and Public Lands@
- Pollution *(204)*
- Recycling@
- Reference *(12)*
- Regional Information *(51)*
- Sustainable Development *(361)* NEW!

Explore the subtopics in a general topic category, or use the keyword search capability only in that topic category.

tools, allowing you to type in a word or words and generate a list of sites that may relate to that topic. One of the major problems with using keyword search engines for research, however, is that the number of sites and documents on almost any topic is so immense that the number of hits or potential resources located for a keyword can run into the thousands. Alternatively, for an uncommon topic, you might receive no hits at all. This problem led to the development of subject indexes, which divide Web resources into broad categories, such as education, health, and so on. Most of the general search engines also have subject indexes. All subject indexes are hierarchical, with major directories connecting to subdirectories and most also offer a keyword search mechanism within subject categories, so after you have narrowed a topic somewhat, you can type in a keyword and search in only part of the database.

Most of the keyword engines allow you to do more sophisticated searches than simply entering one or two key words. Unfortunately, the advanced search features vary widely from one engine to another. Generally, however, the engines offer a help screen that gives instructions on how to customize a search. These are some common search features:

> QUOTATION MARKS—Some of the search engines allow you to put search strings in quotes, indicating that those words must appear in that order in the text. If you are looking for sites about radioactive waste, you could put the words in quotation marks "radioactive waste." Many search engines will recognize proper names, however, so you may not need to put quotation marks around *William Faulkner* if you are searching for information about that author.
>
> PLUS AND MINUS SIGNS—Place a plus (+) in front of a word, and all hits will include that word. Place a minus (–) in front, and none of the hits will include the word.
>
> BOOLEAN OPERATORS—You use words such as *and* and *not* to limit your search. For example, if you use the keywords *radioactive waste*, some of the search engines will return hits for either *radioactive* or *waste*. If you type *radioactive and waste*, however, the search engine will look for those two terms together. If you use the keywords *Shakespeare and not plays* you will receive hits about Shakespeare but not his plays.

Most of the general search engines give you some kind of a description with each hit, rather than just the site name and the Web address. And most return hits in order of relevancy (as perceived by an automated program). So, even if you receive a large number of hits, a few minutes spent perusing them will generally result in finding helpful sites.

Major General Search Engines

ALTAVISTA

http://www.altavista.com

This is one of the most comprehensive search engines, indexing over 250 million Web pages. Alta Vista is a full-text index that searches the entire HTML file, not just the title, and it supports both simple and advanced searches. A good standby, but not a particularly innovative search engine.

ASK JEEVES

http://www.ask.com

Ask Jeeves lets you type in a real question, rather than a series of key words, and it tries to link you to a page that can answer your question. If it can't find an answer for you in its own database, it will provide Web pages from several other search engines.

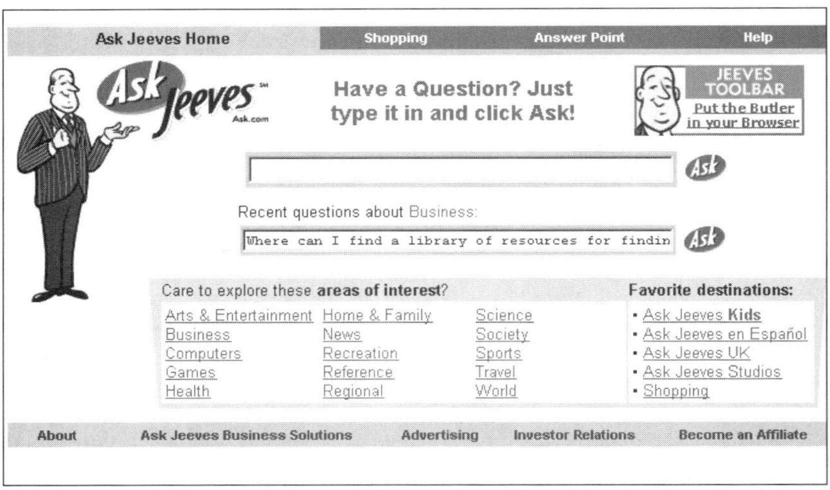

EXCITE

http://www.excite.com

Excite indexes 250 million pages and media objects, and also indexes Usenet newsgroups which can be a great resource for up-to-the-minute research. If you find a page listed on Excite that meets your research needs, you can click on a link to "find similar pages," a tool that allows you to try key words that you might not have considered for your subject.

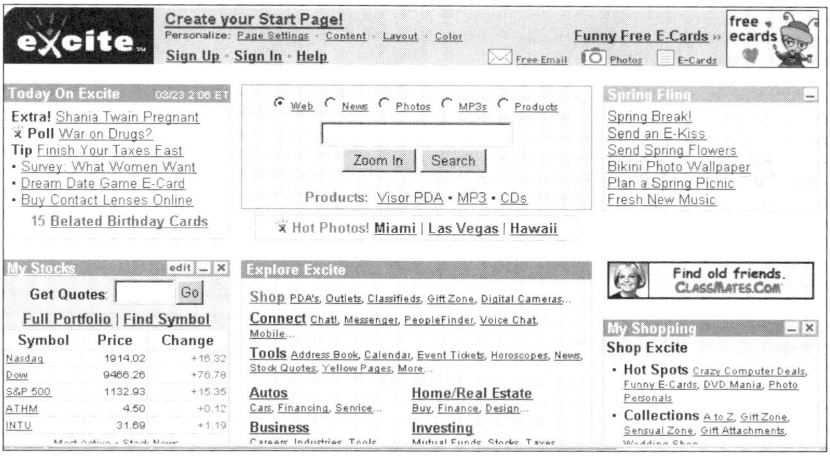

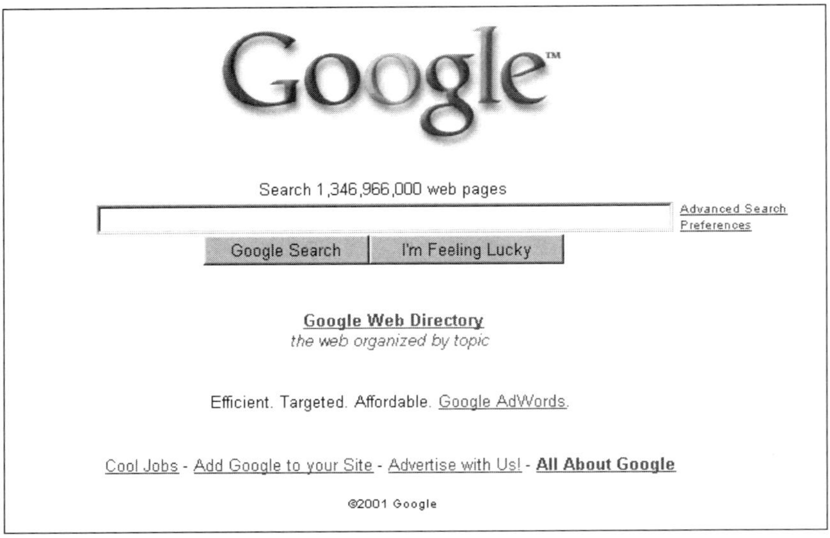

GOOGLE

http://www.google.com

This is a popular search engine which indexes some 1.25 billion web pages. It is a full-text index that searches the entire HTML file. Google has acquired a reputation for scoring hits with high relevancy. This is because it uses link popularity as a way to rank Websites, which means that users "vote" for sites by linking to them, a techniques that works well for general searches.

GO NETWORK (formerly Infoseek)

http://www.go.com

Another popular engine, Go Network, has 75 million sites and is known for its comprehensive coverage and high relevancy of hits. One of the most attractive features about the Go Network is that after each entry, it offers a link to *Similar Pages*. If you find a listing of one useful site, you can use this feature to find others without having to determine what keywords to specify. For more search options, check the welcome screen, usually the first screen you see.

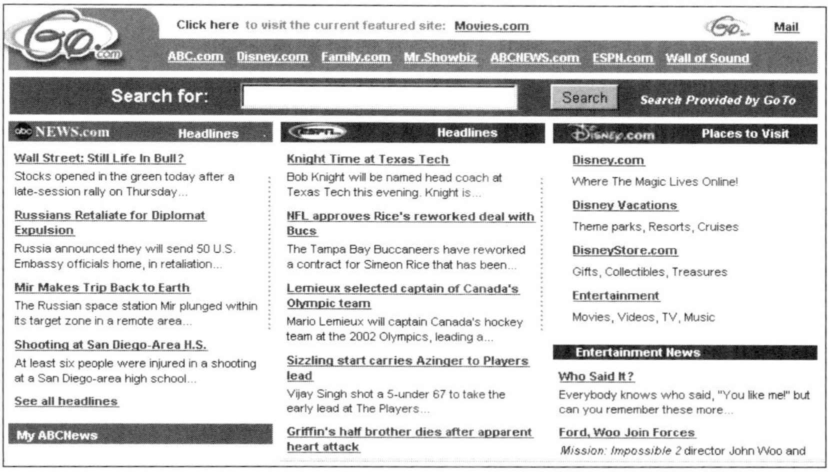

HOTBOT

http://hotbot.lycos.com

HotBot is popular with researchers because of its advanced search options. It relies upon the Open Directory Project and Inktomi databases for its listings. HotBot attempts to be highly comprehensive, and this sometimes causes a problem with deriving hits that are relevant.

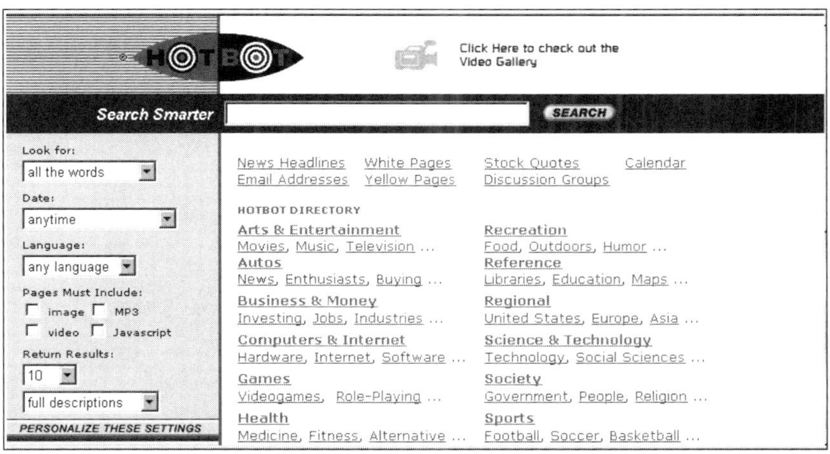

LYCOS

http://www.lycos.com

Lycos was one of the largest of the older search engines on the Web, and it has remained viable because it continues to add new features such as the subject index which is modeled on Yahoo's. Lycos is known for strong relevancy ranking capabilities, and it offers both simple and advanced searching.

OPEN DIRECTORY PROJECT

http://dmoz.org

Open Directory attempts to be the most comprehensive directory of the Web, and it has over 1.8 million listings in a easy-to-use directory format. It relies upon volunteers to catalog Websites.

YAHOO!

http://www.yahoo.com

Yahoo! remains one of the most useful and popular directories on the Web, thanks to its editors who categorize the web. Yahoo has over 1 million sites in its directories which can also be key-word searched. In addition, Yahoo uses Google to supplement its results.

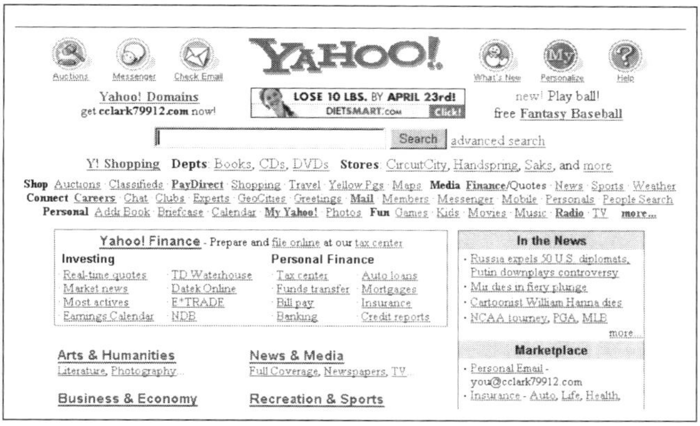

Reproduced with permission of Yahoo! Inc. © 2003 by Yahoo! Inc. YAHOO! and the YAHOO! logo are trademarks of Yahoo! inc.

Sample Search

Keyword Search Engine

Suppose you want to write a paper about radioactive waste. Because you have a defined topic, you can go immediately to one of the keyword search engines such as Google, http://www.google.com. Connecting to Google, you receive a screen that allows you to type in keywords such as *radioactive waste.*

Typing two keywords such as *radioactive* and *waste*, however, is asking the search engine to look for sites that have either word, not both words. In this case, the search engine will return an unmanageable number of hits. You can narrow your search by using quote marks around the words "radioactive waste," which tells the search engine that the two words should appear together in that order.

Google, however, provides you a customized form to narrow your search. Click on *Advanced Search* and you will see this screen, which allows you to indicate whether certain topics are relevant to your search or not.

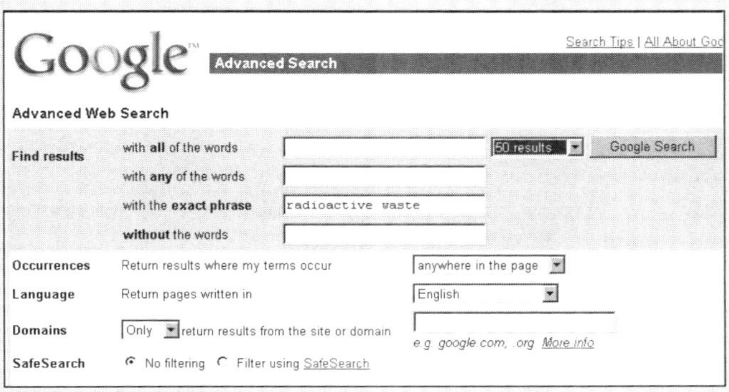

Google is a registered trademark of Google, Inc. All rights reserved. Used with permission.

SELECTED META SEARCH ENGINES

Even the best general search engines only access part of the Web. You can solve this problem by using one of the meta search engines which access several search engines.

Info.com
www.info.com
Searches up to 14 search engines and presents results in groups of twenty, with duplicates included.

Babieca Search
www.babieca.com
Searches 15 search engines and offers the option to control searches and description for listings. Results include redundant entries.

Ixquick
http://www.ixquick.com
Searches 14 search engines, and ranks results by relevancy. Identifies which search engine the entry came from. Supports regular searches, natural language searches, and advanced boolean searches.

Windweaver
www.windweaver.com
Searches 11 popular search engines as well as libraries and directories.

Search Engine Review Sites

If you want to become an expert at finding the most efficient search engines and utilizing them in the most effective ways, check out one of the search engine review sites such as Search Engine Watch, (www.searchenginewatch.com), SearchIQ, (http://www.searchiq.com) or Search Engine Showdown (www.notess.com/search).

MAGAZINES AND NEWSPAPERS

Fortune, the *New York Times*, *Time*, *Wired* magazine—numerous print publications are moving onto the Web, offering full-text articles in special editions or complete Web versions of the print publications. Many also offer search features for the current edition and sometimes for back issues.

Like other resources on the Web, several avenues exist to reach these publications, but no one functional and polished interface accesses all publications you might want to consult. If you know the name of the publication, try locating it directly through one of the keyword search engines.

For magazines and newspapers also try Newsdirectory, http://www.newsdirectory.com. For magazines, look at MagazinesAtoZ.com, http://www.magazinesatoz.com; Magazine Rack, http://www.magazine-rack.com; Yahoo!'s magazine list, http://dir.yahoo.com/News_and_Media/Magazines, which is organized by category, or one of the other search engine's lists of magazines.

For newspapers, try Internet Public Library, http://www.ipl.org/reading/news; OnlineNewspapers.com, http://www.onlinenewspapers.com; Newspapers.com, http://www.newspapers.com; Yahoo!'s list, http://dir.yahoo.com/News_and_Media/Newspapers; or another search engine's list. For U.S. newspapers, try About at http://usnewspapers.about.com/newsissues/usenewspapers

Sample Search

Magazines and Newspapers

Browsing on the Web through a prominent magazine such as *Time* or *Newsweek* may give you ideas for a term paper topic. Or you may already have a topic, and you may want to get a sense of what is going on currently in that subject area. You can connect to *Time* at http://www.time.com and *Newsweek* at http://www.newsweek.com.

If you were looking at the issue of *Newsweek* pictured below, for example, you would see that the Oscars are a hot topic, and it may give you ideas for a term paper about the politics behind the Oscars. You have one article and an idea, so you can now research the Web for more research materials.

Glancing through Newsweek magazines, you might find a topic that interests you.

EXAMPLES OF POPULAR MAGAZINES AND NEWSPAPERS WITH ONLINE EDITIONS

Business Week	http://www.businessweek.com
New York Times	http://www.nytimes.com
Smithsonian Magazine	http://www.smithsonianmag.si.edu
Time	http://www.time.com
USA Today	http://www.usatoday.com
U.S. News Online	http://www.usnews.com/usnews/home.htm
Wired	http://www.wired.com/wired/current.html

LIBRARIES' FULL-TEXT DATABASES

Most college and university libraries offer CD-Rom magazine and newspaper full-text databases on computers in their libraries. Often these same databases are accessible through a library's Web page, though access may be restricted to students and faculty. ProQuest Direct, Periodical Abstracts (via Ovid), FirstSearch, Infotrac, and EBSCOhost are good examples of general databases. More specialized databases are also available in many fields Often, databases index 2000 to 3000 journals, magazines, and/or newspapers; and they are searchable by title, author, and key word. The databases provide bibliographic information, abstracts, and, in many cases, full-text articles.

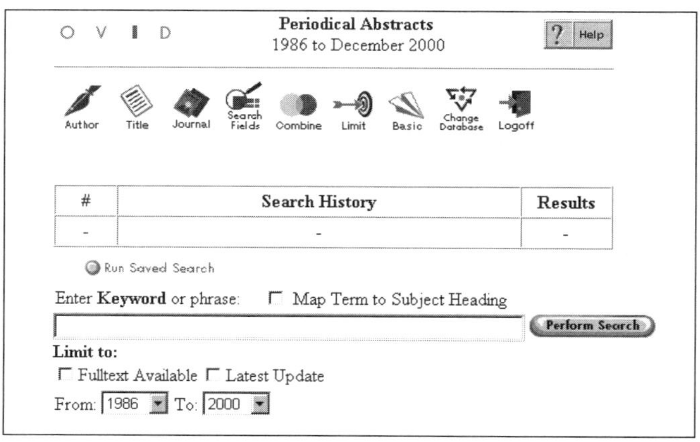

Periodical Abstracts (via Ovid) is one of several full-text databases offering magazine, journal, and newspaper articles through university libraries and their Websites.

Used with permission of Ovid Technologies, Inc.

Librarians' Subject Indexes

One of the best ways to learn about Internet resources is through several indexing projects major libraries sponsor. Librarians have personally reviewed and selected Websites that are of value to academic researchers, including both students and faculty. These indexing Websites are organized by subject area, though most also have keyword search engines as well. You might find it useful to bypass traditional search engines such as Lycos and Excite and to begin research for a term paper with these subject indexes. Thus, you might quickly locate the most authoritative Websites without having to wade through masses of sites looking for the reliable ones. All of these indexes are organized somewhat differently, so you might want to browse through them and select two or three that look user friendly to you.

BUBL LINK

http://bubl.ac.uk/link

BUBL LINK uses the librarian's Dewey Decimal Classification (DDC) to build an Internet subject-oriented resource list. Links are chosen by librarians for their usefulness to academic researchers. The list catalogues over 11,000 resources, a small number compared to search engines, but these are carefully selected resources in all academic disciplines.

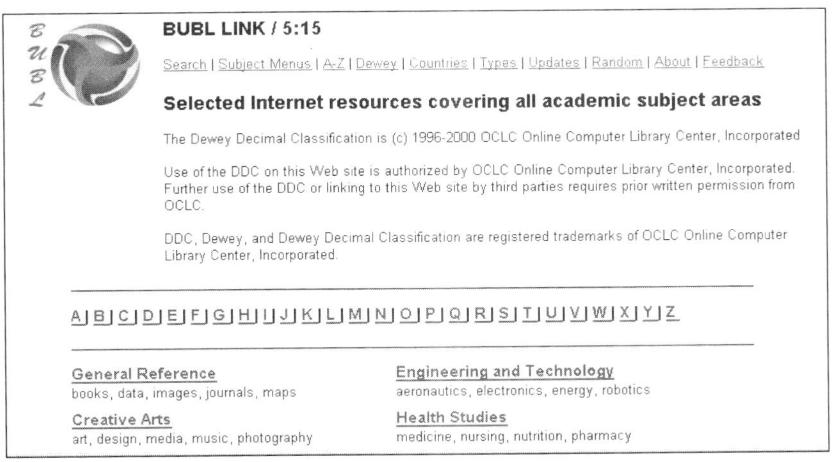

© 2004 BUBL

INFOMINE

http://infomine.ucr.edu

Sponsored by the University of California at Riverside, Infomine offers links to research resources of interest to students and faculty. It is divided into major collections: biological, agricultural, and medical; government information resources; social sciences and humanities (including general reference, business, and library/information studies); physical sciences, engineering, computer science, and mathematics; Internet enabling tools; maps and geographic information systems; visual and performing arts; and instructional resources of the Internet.

INTERNET PUBLIC LIBRARY

http://www.ipl.org

The Reference Center at the Internet Public Library divides Web resources into sections for arts and humanities, sciences and technology, health and medical sciences, law, government and political science, computers and Internet, business and economics, social sciences, and entertainment and leisure. The "Ask a Question" section allows the user to send a query via MOO form or e-mail, and a real librarian will respond to questions with a factual answer or list of resources within 3–7 days. Lists and links to online books and magazines can be found in the Reading Room. The IPL is designed for K-12 students but is also useful for college students.

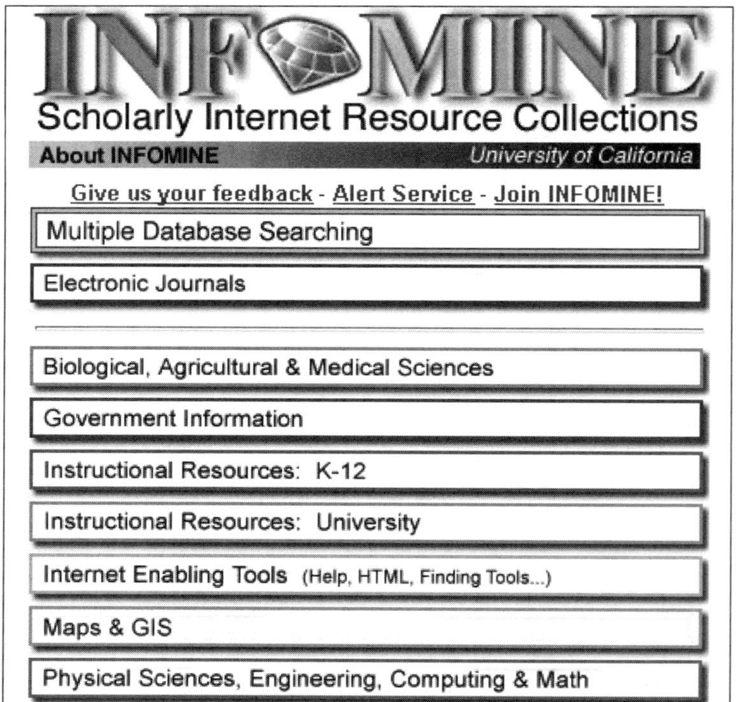

Reprinted by permission with the Regents of the University of California.

INTERNET SCOUT PROJECT

http://scout.wisc.edu

The Internet Scout Project isn't exactly a library project, but numerous librarians and educators are involved in its indexing. Sponsored by the National Science Foundation, the Internet Scout Project offers timely information to the education community about valuable Internet resources. Among its services is the *Scout Report*, a weekly guide to new Internet resources read by some one hundred thousand people. It can be received either by e-mail or read in the Internet Scout Web pages.

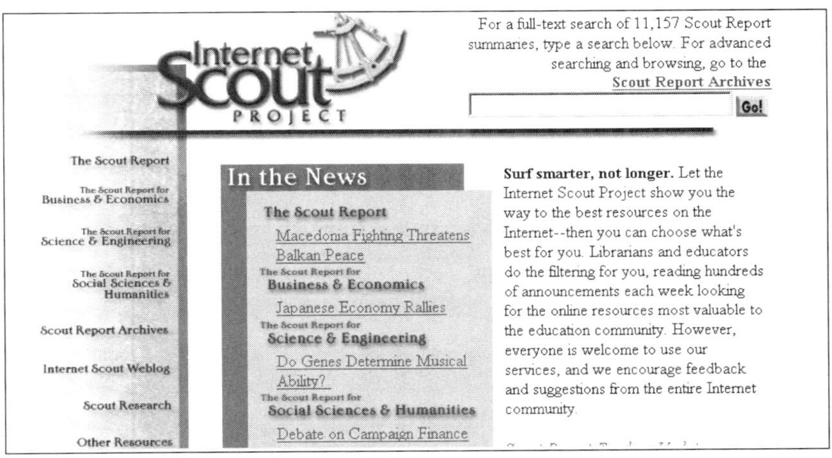

LIBRARIANS' INDEX TO THE INTERNET

http://lii.org/

A searchable subject index, this site lists more than 5000 Internet resources selected and evaluated by librarians at the California State Library. The subject index is arranged in about forty broad categories with subcategories, and the keyword search index has search tips for customized searches. This site is meant to be used by both librarians and non-librarians as a reliable and efficient guide to described and evaluated Internet resources. Supported in part by Federal Library Services and Technology Act finding, it is administered by the California State Library.

MARTINDALES: THE REFERENCE DESK

http://www.martindalecenter.com

Located in Australia, Martindales provides an index to online references, including links to thousands of teaching files, multimedia tutorials, and databases in a wide variety of subjects.

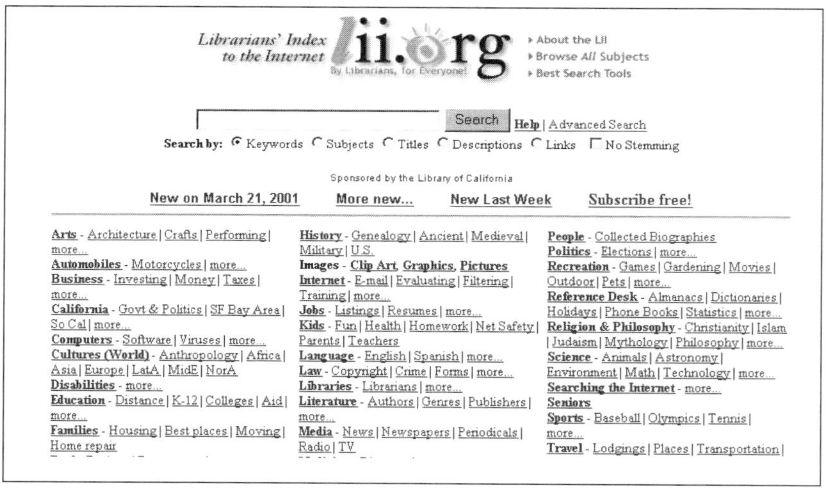

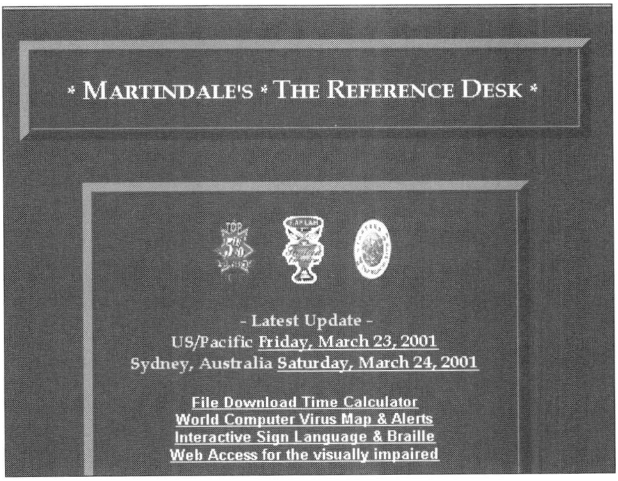

WWW VIRTUAL LIBRARY

http://vlib.org

The WWW Virtual Library is sponsored by CERN, the center for high-energy physics research where the Web was begun. The library is quite extensive, and not all pages are located at CERN. Rather, they are from a collaborative volunteer effort to gather information on a wide variety of topics. The Virtual Library does not offer a keyword search option, but its subject indexes are easy to follow.

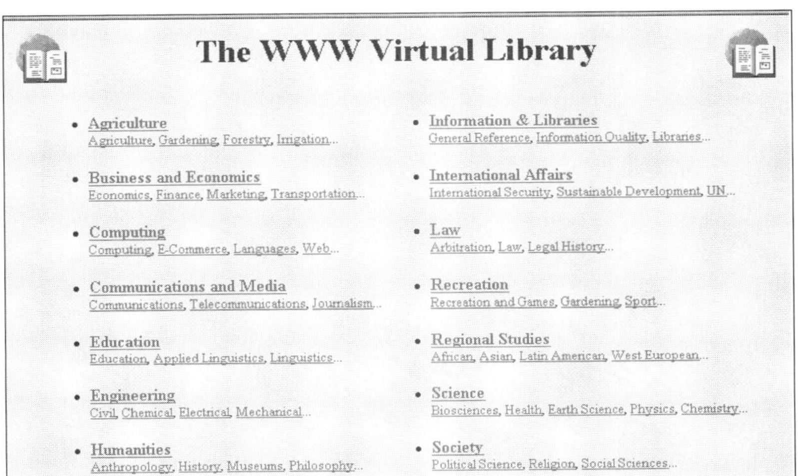

THINGS TO REMEMBER

1. The Web is a fluid medium. What you find today may be gone tomorrow. If you find a useful source, document it thoroughly and keep copies of all of the relevant text portions.
2. If a URL you have doesn't work, do not immediately give up. First, check the address. Web addresses require total accuracy and are uppercase/lowercase sensitive. Often, the pages you are seeking are still on the same computer but have been given a slightly different name. Take the address and cut off the last part. See if that truncated address connects. If it does, look around at the page you find and see if your destination is listed. If this address still does not work, cut off another section and try again.
3. If you are using a search engine, read the directions on the help screens. They will tell you how to customize your search, and this varies widely from one engine to another.
4. Evaluate all material for bias and accuracy. It is very easy to publish on the World Wide Web, and the accuracy of materials varies widely.
5. Be sure to give credit where credit is due. If you find a particular site useful, be sure to reference it in your works cited or reference list.

C H A P T E R 4

Email, Email Discussion Groups, and Newsgroups

Email is the most common use of the Internet, exceeding even exploration of the World Wide Web. As a student, you already may use email to communicate with friends and family across the world or across town. If you haven't been initiated yet into the pleasures of this casual and easy communication form, this chapter will provide you with the basics and some examples of email programs.

Increasingly, email is becoming part of the college classroom. Your instructor may have you submit assignments by email or may suggest that you use it as an alternative way to communicate with him or her. You may find it easier to ask your instructor questions by email than you do in class or in an office visit. You also may have a class email discussion group (sometimes informally called a Listserv) or a class mailing list that you use as a forum for discussion of topics related to your classroom studies.

This chapter discusses and demonstrates the basics of email, email discussion groups, and newsgroups. Email discussion groups are mailing lists that you subscribe to, and you receive messages in your email box from members. A discussion of newsgroups (also called Usenet newsgroups), though not accessed by email, is included in this chapter because it provides communication possibilities similar to email discussion groups. You do not subscribe to newsgroups; rather, you access them through a news reader such as the ones included in Internet Explorer and Netscape Communicator.

In addition to class email discussion groups or newsgroups, you can use public groups as additional avenues for research. This chapter will suggest how to find groups discussing topics relevant to your class research. These groups may include other students or professionals in related fields. When you locate a group that seems relevant, it is a good idea to observe the group discussion for several days before you participate. This is called "lurking." After a few days of reading other people's postings, you will have a good idea of how to participate in the discussion. You may ask, for example, for suggestions about Websites, magazine articles, or books that are particularly relevant to your topic. Or you may find that the group offers opinions you can quote in your research paper. Be aware, however, that information posted in email discussion groups and newsgroups generally is opinion, not verifiable fact.

ANATOMY OF AN EMAIL

An email address looks something like this:

login@serveraddress

An example might be john@unm.edu if John is a student at the University of New Mexico. Or, if John has his email account on a commercial server, his address could look like this:

johnj@instantnet.com.

Thus, all email addresses consist of two parts, the individual's log-in name and the server address. The server address may end in .edu if the email account is on a university-owned server. Commercial servers generally have .com or .net endings to their addresses.

When you obtain your email address, you likely will have some choice about a log-in name. Often the log-in name is some version of the person's real name, though sometimes an arbitrary login is assigned. Some individuals prefer to invent a colorful persona for themselves by creating a unique login name. Choose a login that will be easy to remember, both for your memory's sake and for friends who may want to send you mail. Your login name also may be required to log in to your university's email server, and you probably will be asked to declare a password to protect your account.

EMAIL PROGRAMS

Through many university systems, you can access your email through your Web browser. The following brief discussion tells how to use email programs offered by Internet Explorer, as well as Websites that offer free email hosting. Also included is a brief discussion of Pine, an older email program some universities use. If you do not have access to one of these three programs, however, your email program will function in a similar fashion.

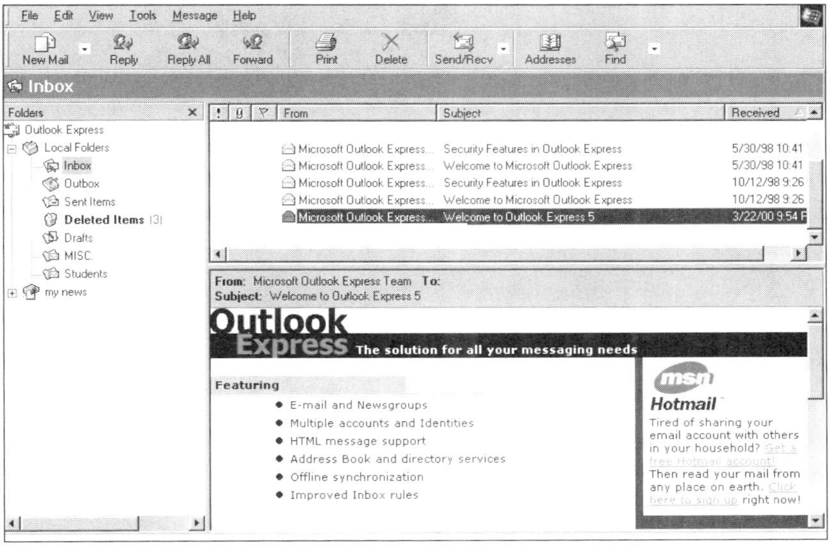

Outlet Express gives you an easy way to send and receive email without leaving the browser.

Internet Explorer Outlook Express

Using Outlook Express with Internet Explorer, you can read your email without leaving the browser. If you want to read your mail, click on the *Mail* icon on the Explorer screen, and choose *Read Mail.* You will see a screen similar to this one:

Your email message will be listed in the upper-right box. You may need to click on *Send and Receive* to download current messages. If you do not have an email or server address indicated in the browser preferences, you may need to specify one, so the browser knows where to locate your email. If you are not prompted by the program to do so, go to the *Tools* menu and select *Accounts.*

Highlight one of your messages by clicking on it, and it will be displayed in the lower right box. After you read the message, you can delete it by clicking *Delete.* You can also save the message in one of your folders listed in the box on the left of the screen. Select the *Edit* menu and choose *Move to Folder.*

If you want to create a message, click on *Compose Message* (or select it from the Explorer main screen by clicking on *New Mail.* The template provides you with spaces for the recipient's email address, any addresses for duplicate copies, a subject line, and attachments. Compose your message in the large box in the lower portion of the screen. When you have finished, you can check your spelling by going to the *Tools* menu. Send your message by clicking *Send.*

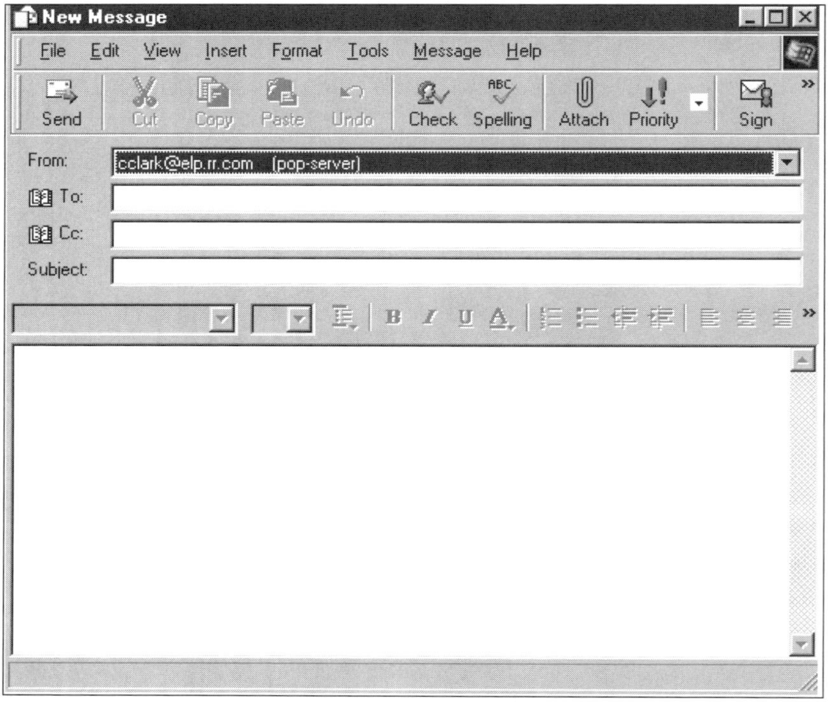

To create a new message in Outlet Express, follow the directions in the template in the top part of the screen and compose your message in the bottom portion.

Outlook Express has many more features you can use to enhance your email communication. Learn about them by exploring the information available through the *Help* menu.

Free Email Hosting Sites

Many Websites offer free email hosting as a way of attracting users to their pages. The appearance and commands of these email programs will vary somewhat, but all will let you read your incoming mail and offer a template for composing and sending new email messages. Generally, you have to register with the site and disclose some demographical information such as income and age which the site can use for marketing.

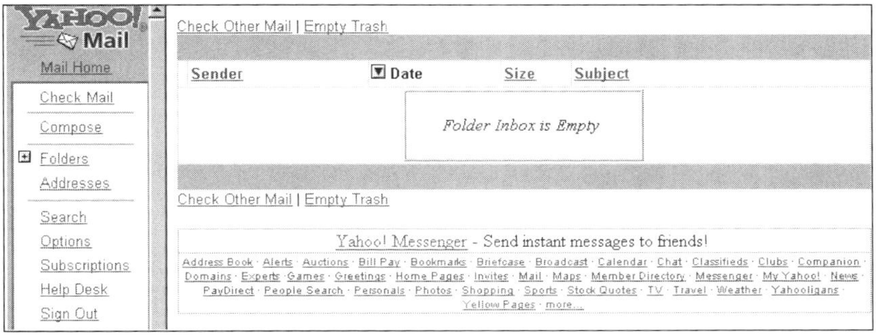

Yahoo is one example of a Website which offers free email hosting.

Pine

An older but efficient email program, Pine is used by many colleges and community organizations that offer text-only access to the Internet. Typically, you access Pine through a menu option when you dial your university's Internet number, or you may Telnet to it (information Telnet allows you to log in to a remote computer network and use its programs). Ask your lab assistant or instructor how to connect to Pine if that is the program available. You will be asked for your log-on information (email address) and a password. Then you will see a welcome screen something like this:

```
?    HELP              -   Get help using Pine
C    COMPOSE MESSAGE   -   Compose and send a message
I    FOLDER INDEX      -   View messages in current folder
L    FOLDER LIST       -   Select a folder to view
A    ADDRESS BOOK      -   Update address book
S    SETUP             -   Configure or update Pine
Q    QUIT              -   Exit the Pine program
```

Pine offers an email option for text-only access to the Internet.

Pine is a menu-driven program with clearly displayed commands and shortcut keys. To compose a message, for example, use your arrow keys to highlight *Compose Message* and press *Enter*. You will see a screen where you can write your email message.

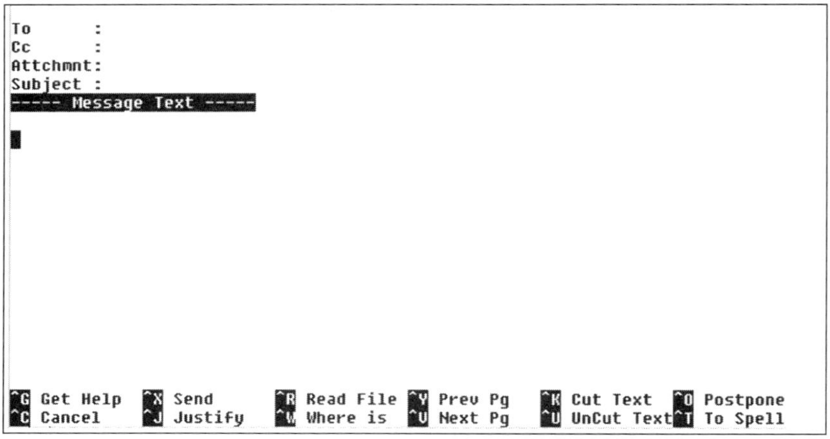

Pine provides a memo-format template for composing an email message.
Reprinted with permission from Martindale-Hubbell, a Division of Reed-Elsevier, Inc.

Notice the list of commands across the bottom of the screen. You can use them to print, spell check, and so forth. To save, for example, press *Control-S*.

To read your mail, select *Folder List* from the opening menu, and press *Enter*. You will see a folder called *Inbox*. Highlight it, and press *Enter* again. You will see a list of your email messages if you have received any. Highlight the email message you want to read, press *Enter*, and you will see the message displayed.

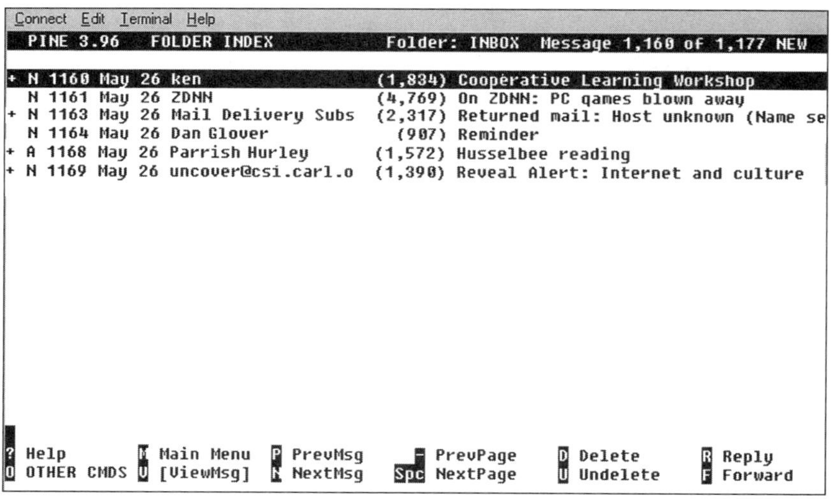

In Pine, the list of email messages look something like this.

Group Discussion via Email and Usenet Newsgroups

Thousands of people communicate every day with others of like interests through two types of discussion groups on the Internet: email discussion groups and newsgroups. The general format of both types is the same. One person sends a message (you can also call it a *posting*) about a topic, which you can identify by the message's subject line. Other people respond about that topic, using the same or similar subject lines and giving their own viewpoint or information. This generates a discussion *thread* or group of posting about the same topic. Threads may last days, weeks, or years, and one discussion group may have numerous threads going at the same time.

You subscribe to email discussion groups, and the postings come to your mailbox. You access newsgroups differently, by connecting to a part of your server that stores the postings of newsgroups. Newsgroups (which may not have anything to do with news or current events) are also called Usenet newsgroups. Both types of discussion groups predate the World Wide Web, though you can access them now through the Web with either Netscape or Explorer. You also can access both types in other ways. Any email program will serve just as well for email discussion groups, and other newsgroup readers are available that do not access newsgroups through the Web.

Email Discussion Groups

(Also Called Listservs or Mailing Lists)

Whether you are interested in discussing current events, accounting for small businesses, or freedom of speech, an email discussion group (sometimes called Listservs or mailing lists) probably exists that matches your interests. Some groups require members to meet certain criteria, such as membership in a college class or having a certain type of degree, but the majority of groups are open to the public. You subscribe to an email discussion group by sending a message to an address managed by an automated program (usually Listserv, Majordomo, or Listproc). Generally, the program subscribes you to the list, sends you a welcome message, and then you begin receiving the group's discussion in the form of email messages members post.

Subscribe and Unsubscribe Commands

Commands such as *subscribe* or *unsubscribe* are sent directly to the list server. Usually that address looks something like this:

listserv@domainname

Listserv-type programs are generally case insensitive, which means you can type *Listserv* or *listserv* and the program will respond to either. If the Listserv address is listserv@xuniversity.edu, you would put that address on the *To*: line of your email message. Other programs utilize addresses similar to majordomo@xcompany.com or listname-request@xcompany.com. Use whatever address you have been given for the group. Leave the subject line blank.

In the message body, you will need to give a subscribe command. These vary slightly depending on which program the server is running, but generally they follow this format:

> Subscribe command: subscribe [listname] [firstname lastname]
> Unsubscribe command: unsubscribe [listname]

For example, if you were subscribing to a Listproc discussion group called apple-1, your message might read:

Subscribe apple-1 James Moffit

After the automated program receives your request for subscription, you will receive a message informing you of commands to use and other information the group wishes subscribers to have. It is a good idea to save this message, for you may want to refer to it later.

Posting Messages to a Group

To post, you send your message to an entirely different address than the one you used to subscribe. Usually the address looks like this:

listname@domainname

You will find the posting address among the directions in your welcome message from the group. Do include a subject line, for many participants may decide whether or not to read a message from what the subject line indicates about the message.

Finding Interesting Groups

Several Websites now offer searchable lists of email discussion groups. Connect to one of these sites, and follow the directions for using its search features to find groups in your area of interest:

CataList

http://www.lsoft.com/lists/listref.html

Liszt

http://www.liszt.com

Directory of Scholarly E-Conferences

http://www.n2h2.com/KOVACS

Publicly Accessible Mailing Lists

http://paml.net

You also can do an email keyword search for a group focusing on a particular topic. Send a message to listserv@listserv.net (or another Listserv maintaining a list of Listservs) including the keywords. The message would look like this:

list global [keywords]

If, for example, you were interested in a group discussing campus conditions, you might use the message list global campus. You would receive a list of email discussion groups with that keyword, and the list would look something like this:

```
ACAA          ACAA@LISTSERV.UIC.EDU
        The Association of Campus Activities Administrators

ACPBEXEC      ACPBEXEC@LISTSERV.KENT.EDU
        Email the executive board of the All Campus Programming Board

ADS           ADS@UPE.AC.ZA
        Adverts on campus

ADVISING-L    ADVISING-L@LISTS.SUNYSB.EDU
        Professional advisors in all divisions of campus.

AGAPEHOUSE    AGAPEHOUSE@LISTSERV.UIC.EDU
        United Campus Ministry at UIC

AGGIEUCM      AGGIEUCM@LISTSERV.TAMU.EDU
        United Campus Ministries in Aggieland

AM-OCAEXEC    AM-OCAEXEC@LISTSERV.TAMU.EDU
        Off Campus Aggies Exec Staff

ANNOUNCE      ANNOUNCE@UMR.EDU
        UMR Campus Computing Services Announcements

AUTHENTICATION-L AUTHENTICATION-L@LISTSERV.UCLA.EDU
        UCLA campus authentication discussion
```

This group list of Email discussion groups having to do with "campus" was obtained from listserv@listserv.net.

Used with permission from L-Soft from www.lsoft.com

NEWSGROUPS

Though the function of newsgroups (sometimes called Usenet newsgroups) is similar in many ways to email discussion groups, they vary in how you access them. As noted earlier, you subscribe to email discussion groups, and the messages come to your mailbox. Newsgroup messages, in contrast, are collected at a central location. You connect to a particular group your Internet provider has subscribed to and read selected messages. An advantage of newsgroups is that the messages are never downloaded to your email, so they do not clog your in-box. On the other hand, you have to develop the habit of checking your group messages, or you do not get the benefits of participating in a group discussion.

Newsgroups are broken into categories that are indicated by a prefix to the name of the group. The most common prefixes are

alt	alternative—broad range of topics
biz	business
comp	computers, computer science
misc	other
news	news about newsgroups
rec	recreation and hobbies
sci	scientific
soc	social issues
talk	debate

The prefix is followed by one or more specific subject names. For example, news.newusers.questions is a group that answers questions from new participants in newsgroups.

Reading Newsgroups in Internet Explorer

To access newsgroups in Internet Explorer, go the *Mail* menu and select *Read News*. If you are using Microsoft Outlook Express as your newsgroup reader, your screen will appear like the one here.

In the box on the left side you will find listed the newsgroups you are subscribed to. If you click on the name of one of the groups, it will display a list of unread messages in the top right box. Click on a message, and it will appear in the lower right box. In this example, the group *news.announce.newusers* is highlighted, a group where announcements are posted about newsgroups. Select a message, and it will appear in the lower box on the right.

If you have no groups listed in the box on the right of the screen or if you want to subscribe to additional groups, click on *News groups*. You will receive this box, where you can review newsgroups your provider has subscribed to:

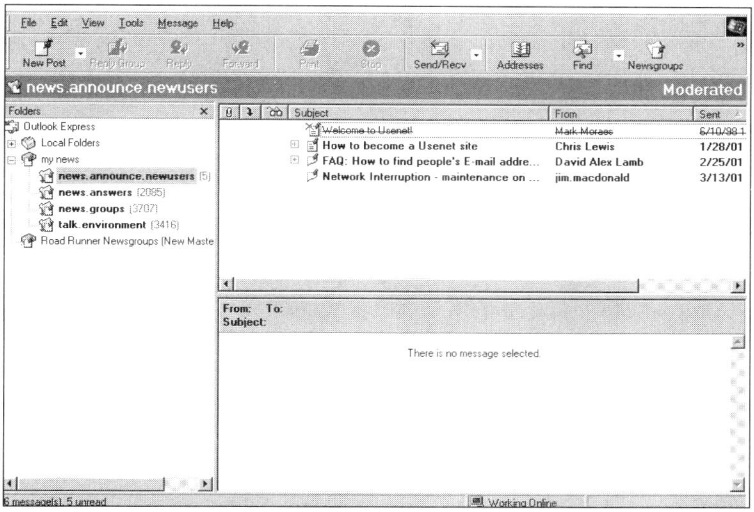

Internet Explorer provides a built-in news reader.

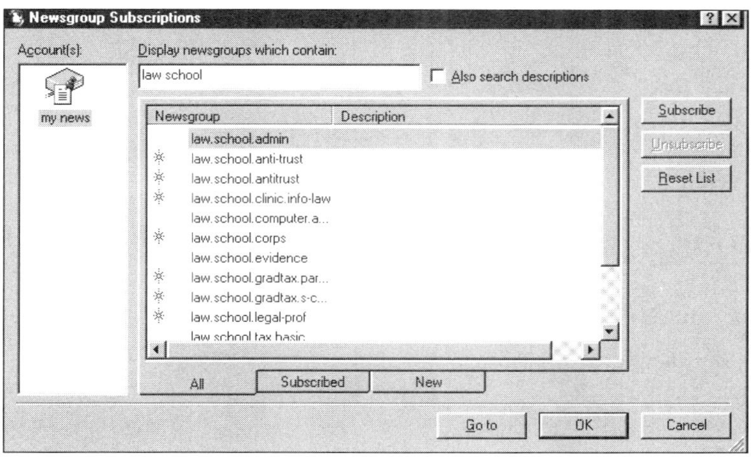

Outlet Express allows you to search newsgroups by key word.

You can type in a keyword in the box, and Outlook Express will list the groups that include that keyword in the name of their group. In the screen illustrated, the words *law school* were entered, and groups are listed that include that word. You can then decide to subscribe to one or more groups.

When you have a group selected and you want to post a message to it, click on *New Post*. If you want to reply to a posted message, click on *Reply Group*. If you want to send a message only to the author of the message you have been reading, click on *Reply*. In each case, you will receive a box where you can type your message; then click on *Send*, which you will find in the *File* menu.

Finding Relevant Groups

As described previously, news-reading software such as Internet Explorer have a keyword search function that can be used to find groups, but this will not work for groups that use abbreviations for their names. Try a keyword search at one of the sources for group archives and information, such as Google (formerly DejaNews archive) at http://www.google.com, Liszt's Usenet Newsgroups Directory at http://www.liszt.com/news, Usenet Info Center Launch Pad at http://www.ibiblio.org/usenet-i, or Cyberfiber, http://www.cyberfiber.com. You can locate the name of a group in the archives and then access newsgroups through your browser and read what is going on currently with the same group.

CHAPTER 5

DOCUMENTING INTERNET SOURCES

To use the extensive resource materials available on the World Wide Web in research projects, you must document your sources. This allows your audience, should they be interested, to retrace your research steps and look at the materials you have used. To do this, you need to provide references in the text to the materials you have used and at the end of your paper furnish a works-cited or reference page. Be aware, however, that Web addresses change and sources sometimes disappear. It is advisable to print out or save on disk any reference material crucial to your research. You can, thus, continually refer to the material, and you can, if necessary, provide a copy for your instructor.

Because the use of Internet sources has grown so quickly, conventions for documenting Web sources are still developing. Check with your professor first about his or her preferences for documenting online sources. You may find handbooks or sites on the Web that suggest somewhat different approaches to documentation of Web sources. This chapter offers models for citing sources that are consistent with Modern Language Association (MLA) and American Psychological Association (APA) styles.

MODERN LANGUAGE ASSOCIATION STYLE

For MLA style, also refer to the *MLA Handbook for Writers of Research Papers* and the MLA Website, http://www.mla.org.

In-Text Citation

Modern Language Association style uses parenthetical (in-text) references that are keyed to a works-cited page at the end of the paper. For print sources, the name of the author and the page number provide the references. This type of citation is difficult for Web sources because few have page numbers, and many do not have specified authors. If you have an author and page or section number, give them. If no author is specified, use a shortened part of the title of the text.

EXAMPLE

According to an *Internet World* article, "Job Trak, the nation's leading online job listing service, claims to have already been used by more than a million students and alumni, with more than 150,000 employers and 300 college career centers posting new jobs daily" (Grusky).

Works-Cited Page

Ideally, a works-cited page provides sufficient information about all the sources you have used so that your readers can locate the materials should they wish to do so. For Web sources, pages change or disappear; thus, you need to include the date you accessed the site in addition to any publication date the source specified.

These are some examples of typical documents you might need to reference:

1. **Book:**

   Give both the date of publication and the date of access.

   Reilly, Bernard F., Jr., *Library of Congress Prints and Photographs: An Illustrated Guide with a Preface by Stephen E. Ostrow.* Washington: Library of Congress, 1995. Library of Congress. 24 March 2001 <http://www.loc.gov/rr/print/guide>.

2. **An article in a magazine:**

   Give both the date of publication and the date of access.

   Baird, Sara. "Mom's a Head-Banger." *Salon.* 7 Oct. 1977. 20 March 2001 <http://www.salonmagazine.com/mwt/feature/1997/10/07rock.html>

3. **A journal article:**

   Kraut, Robert, & Lundmark, Vicki (1998). "Internet Paradox: A Social Technology That Reduces Social Involvement and Psychological Well-Being?" *American Psychologist* 53 (1998): 22 March 2001 <http://www.apa.org/journals/amp/amp5391017.html>

4. **Professional Website:**

   Virtual Computer Library. U of Texas. 22 March 2001 <http://www.utexas.edu/computer/vcl>

5. **Commercial Website page:**

   Vacation and Last-minute Specials. American Express. 24 March 2001 <http://travel.americanexpress.com/travel/lmt/default.asp?bcid=1&lmt=1_home=travlastmin>

6. **Personal Website:**

   Barlow, John Perry. Home page. 22 March 2001 <http://www.eff.org/%7Ebarlow/barlow.html>.

7. **Scholarly project:**

   Rhetoric and Composition. 29 Nov. 1996. University of Washington. 24 March 2001. <http://eserver.org/rhetoric>

8. **Article in a subscription database:**

   Linn, Susan. "Sellouts." *American Prospect*. 23 Oct. 2000: 17-20. *Periodical Abstracts*. University of Texas at El Paso Library, El Paso, TX. 15 March 2001 <http://libraryweb.utep.edu/eriodicalabatracts>

American Psychological Association Style

For APA style, also refer to the *Publication Manual of the American Psychological Association* and the APA Website, http://www.apastyle.org/

In-Text Citations

American Psychological Association style specifies giving the author and date after referenced material in the text and giving author, date, and page numbers after quotations. This type of citation is difficult for Web sources because many texts do not have specified authors or dates of publication. If you have an author and date of publication, give them. If no author is specified, use a shortened part of the title of the text.

EXAMPLE

According to an *Internet World* article, "Job Trak, the nation's leading online job listing service, claims to have already been used by more than a million students and alumni, with more than 150,000 employers and 300 college career centers posting new jobs daily" (Grusky, 1996).

The APA also suggests citing Website home pages by giving the address in the text (e.g., http://www.apa.org). No citation on the reference page is needed. For specific articles posted on the World Wide Web, always cite the article in the reference list and include "retrieved from" and the date.

Reference List

Instead of a works-cited page, APA specifies a reference list. Since you can cite Web page addresses in the text, according to the APA Web page, you would put Web references in the reference list only if they refer to specific articles or books published on the World Wide Web.

EXAMPLES

Kraut, R., & Lundmark, V. (1998). Internet paradox: A social technology that reduces social involvement and psychological well-being? *American Psychologist,* 53, pp. 1017-1031. Retrieved April 15, 2000, from the World Wide Web: http://www.apa.org/journals/amp/amp5391017.html

Electronic reference formats recommended by the American Psychological Association. (2001, January 10). Washington, DC: American Psychological Association. Retrieved March 22, 2001, from the World Wide Web: http://www.apa.org/journals/webref.html

Article in an electronic database

Linn, S. (2000, Oct. 23) Sellouts. *American Prospect,* 11(22), pp. 17-20. Retrieved March 15, 2001, from *Periodical Abstracts* database, accession number 62528011, on the World Wide Web: http://libraryweb.utep.edu/periodicalabatracts

PART I APPENDIX

SOURCES OF ADDITIONAL INFORMATION

GENERAL INTERNET/WEB GUIDES

The Complete Internet Guide and Web Tutorial
http://www.microsoft.com/insider/internet

WebNovice
http://www.webnovice.com

Beginners' Central
http://www.northernwebs.com/bc

Exploring the World-Wide Web
http://www.gactr.uga.edu/exploring/index.html

Virtual Computer Library
http://www.utexas.edu/computer/vcl

World Wide Web FAQ
http://www.boutell.com/faq

The World Wide Web for the Clueless
http://www.mit.edu/people/rei/wwwintro.html

Recommended Internet Search Engines & Finding Tools
http://infomine.ucr.edu/guides/index

Internet Search Tool Details
http://sunsite.berkeley.edu/Help/searchdetails.html

WebPlaces Internet Search Guide
http://www.webplaces.com

SEARCH ENGINE GUIDES AND REVIEWS

Search Engine Watch
http://www.searchenginewatch.com

Search Engine Showdown
http://www.notess.com/search

PART II

WWW.THOMSON.COM/LEARNING

Thomson Learning Accounting Website Overview

Thomson Learning Website Navigation

Introduction to Accounting Topics

Thomson Learning Accounting Website Overview

Thomson Learning Website Navigation

This section will help you learn more about Thomson Learning's Website, acquaint you with what is available, where to find it, and how to make it work for you.

Thomson Learning's home page offers both instructors and students the opportunity to discover more about our parent company, Thomson Learning, as well as the many areas of interest from High School Advanced Placement materials to information regarding International Colleges and Universities.

If you know what you want but are unsure where to find it on the site, use the **Search us** tool provided on the home page. This allows you to type in the topic you are looking for and generates a number of possible links to your area of interest.

- About us links to a brief history of Thomson Learning.
- Contact us provides information on how to provide feedback, review employment opportunities, and submit future proposal ideas.
- Shop us links you directly to our E-store where you can purchase lab manuals, educational software, study guides, and other material not always found in bookstores.

Another way to navigate the Thomson Learning Website is to use the tabs at the top of the home page. Each tab represents a particular page of services to our customers.

- The **E-service** tab represents Thomson Learning's customer relation services from where to find a subject/book to site concerns, like quizzing issues or technical support.
- The **Instructors** tab provides information and tools where instructors can purchase material for their course and develop course syllabi or quizzes.
- The **Students** tab provides you with quick links to tools and information like study aids, online quizzes, and review material.

On the top of the home page click the **Students** tab for more information written and designed with the student in mind. Links to free interactive study aids, like **Gimme-An-A,** help you prepare for exams, take course quizzes, and boost your understanding of key course concepts. Our Students tab also offers easy access to online **Career Resources,** including job listings and résumé tips.

Not only have we created a page that provides links to tools and valuable study material, you can also search for important information regarding your course's appropriate textbook via **Find A Subject/Book Site.**

Within each discipline, or area of study, you will find more detailed information regarding the textbook.

INTRODUCTION TO ACCOUNTING TOPICS

The Thomson Learning Web site for Accounting (http://www.swcollege.com/acct/accounting.html) provides resources that help you:

- Understand your current course in Accounting
- Learn about the academic and professional fields of Accounting

Here is an overview of what you will find on the site:

- FIND YOUR TEXTBOOK! Click on the "By Course" icon to find information and support resources associated with the book you are currently using, books you will use in other courses, and additional course-related material in the following areas:

- Accounting Ethics
- Accounting Information Systems
- Accounting Principles
- Accounting Theory
- Advanced Accounting
- Auditing
- Auditing Research
- Auditing and Assurance
- College Accounting
- Computerized Accounting
- Corporate Financial Accounting
- Cost Accounting
- Cost Management
- Financial & Managerial Accounting
- Financial Accounting
- Financial Statement Analysis
- Forensic Accounting
- Intermediate Accounting
- International Accounting
- Introduction to E-Commerce
- Management Accounting
- Managerial Accounting
- MBA Accounting
- Payroll Accounting
- Survey of Accounting

✦ RESOURCE CENTER. Click on the following links on the "How may we help you?" drop-down menu for students to find additional Accounting resources:

- COST ACCOUNTING SUPPLEMENTS: Explore topic modules prepared for use in managerial accounting courses. This on-line product reviews most major managerial topics in a convenient, user-friendly manner.
- MANAGERIAL ACCOUNTING SUPPLEMENTS
- MBA TITLES
- ACCOUNTING LINKS: Online resources to enhance the Accounting learning experience.

- INTERESTED IN A CAREER IN ACCOUNTING? Follow these links to information about current job openings, career opportunities, tools and techniques for landing a job.

PART III

ACCOUNTING WEBSITES

HITS Hottest Accounting Sites on the Web

Accounting Educational/Research

Accounting Fun

Accounting Careers

HITS HOTTEST ACCOUNTING SITES ON THE WEB

ACCOUNTING EDUCATIONAL/RESEARCH

AACSB -- The International Association for Management Education

This is the site for the accrediting body for programs in business admisnistration, management, and acounting. It supplies links to Management Education markets for both employers and job seekers, and to information about member services.

http://www.aacsb.edu/

The Academy of Accounting Historians

The Academy of Accounting Historians encourages research, publication, teaching, and personal interchanges in all phases of Accounting History and its interrelation with business and economic history. Its website is a resource for links to accounting journals, organizations, career services, educational institutions, and other resources for accountants.

http://accounting.rutgers.edu/raw/aah/

Accountancy in Europe

The homepage for the Social Science Information Gateway (SOSIG) offers internet resources (listed by type) in accounting, education and research, and related subjects for Europe and the UK. These resources offer social scientists a tool for finding Accountancy information to support their work.

http://www.sosig.ac.uk/business/accounting_profession/

Accountant-Finder

The site is an "accountant directory" for the world, including various categories of accounting. Links provided enable the researcher to find accountants, consultants, services, and other accounting resources.

http://www.cpafinder.com/

Accountant's Home Page

The Accountant's Home Page is a guide to accounting sites, a "launching point" for accountants searching for Internet resources. This site provides links to resources such as accountants, data bases, banking sites, software, and others of interest.

http://www.computercpa.com/

Accounting

This web site accompanies Accounting, the best-selling accounting textbook which has helped over 11 million students learn and countless numbers of teachers teach. Included are sites to accompany this and other textbooks by Warren, Reeve, and Fees, and published by South-Western. The site includes Instructor Resources, Interactive Study Center, Student Resources, and more links.

http://www.swcollege.com/acct/warren/warren_choose.htm

Accounting, Auditing, and Accountability Journal

Published by the MCB University Press, the AAAJ online is a resource for academics seeking knowledge of accounting practices from an historical perspective. The site offers links to manuscripts concerning accounting/auditing in a socio-economic and political framework.

http://www.mcb.co.uk/aaaj.htm

Accounting: A Virtual History

This site for the Association of Chartered Accountants seeks to answer the question "Why study accounting history?" The site provides a brief history of accounting, and links for further history and information, including a bookstore and library.

http://www.acaus.org/acc_his.html

Accounting Hall of Fame

The Accounting Hall of Fame honors accountants who have made or are making a significant contribution to the advancement of accounting since the beginning of the twentieth century. Links provided include those to the year's inductees, and alphabetical and chronological lists of members.

http://fisher.osu.edu/acctmis/hall/index.htm

Accounting History Page

This site provides a rationale for studying accounting history and offers works by Gary Giroux, including an outline and summary of his work in progress. The site also provides "Links to the Past" in accounting and business, museums, companies, individuals, and other historical sites.

http://acct.tamu.edu/giroux/history.html

Accounting Research Network

The Accounting Research Network (ARN) publishes abstracts of top quality research papers in three journals in an effort to increase communication among accounting scholars and practitioners. The site offers links to the journals, as well as to professional announcements and job openings, and related accounting networks.

http://www.ssrn.com/arn/index.html

Activity Based Cost

The site is essentially an article by Edwin B. Dean which explains ABC, a tool for cost management. The site offers a rationale for ABC, and gives a review of related publications on activity-based costing. It also includes bibliographies.

http://techreports.larc.nasa.gov/ltrs/PDF/aiaa-92-1057.pdf

Advancing Government Accountability

The Association of Government Accountants maintains this site, which offers membership into the association, as well as links to publications, including the AGA Journal, relating to government accounting. The site also offers an online course in government accounting.

http://www.agacgfm.org

American Accounting Association

The AAA is a voluntary organization of persons interested in accounting education and research. The AAA web site provides links to news, marketplaces, publications, and organizations in accounting, in addition to membership information.

http://aaahq.org/index.cfm

Association of Latino Professionals in Finance and Accounting

The purpose of ALPHA is to help Latinos in accounting and finance professions. The website provides links to career opportunities, contacts, and scholarships for Latinos in accounting and finance, as well as membership information.

http://www.alpfa.org

American Institute of Certified Public Accountants

The AICPA is a national professional organization for CPAs in the U.S. The site provides a search engine, in addition to career opportunities, accounting news, resources, and products, as well as information on The Journal of Accountancy.

http://www.aicpa.org/

American Society of Women Accountants

The ASWA exists to increase opportunities for women in all fields of accounting and finance. Links provided by this web site include membership information, an Internet directory to membership services, and employment opportunities.

http://www.aswa.org

Arthur Andersen

This site offers a description of the Arthur Andersen Company, one of the Big Five Accounting firms. Included are links to market offerings in the U.S. and abroad, careers, and resources such as books, news events, and research in accounting.

http://www.arthurandersen.com/

Beta Alpha Psi

The site for BAP, a professional accounting and business fraternity, provides links for membership availability, career opportunities, community service, in addition to links of interest in accounting and business information.

http://www.cob.fsu.edu/students/orgs/bap/

Bond Market Association

This association represents securities firms and banks which underwrite, trade, and sell debt securities. The home page includes tools and links for research into statistics and reports, as well as policy and advocacy in, among other things, market practices and regulatory and e-commerce issues.

http://www.bondmarkets.com/

British Accounting Review

This journal is a forum for communication throughout the world between members of academic and professional communities concerned with the research and teaching of accounting, finance, and related disciplines. The site offers an explanation of journal articles, and research and database coverage.

http://www.academicpress.com/bar

CA Magazine

This is the official publication of the Canadian Institute of Chartered Accountants. The information on the publication's site includes chartered accountants profession documents for comment, products and services, and standards and guidance in the field.

http://www.cica.ca/index.cfm/ci_id/17150/la_id/1.htm

CMA Canada

The site for the Society of Management Accountants of Canada, a North American organization for financial and strategic professionals, offers links to business publications, career opportunities, and news updates. Information about the organization is also included.

http://www.cma-canada.org/

College Accounting

This web site accompanies the textbook Accounting, by Heintz/Parry and published by South-Western. The site includes Instructor Resources, Interactive Study Center, Student Resources, and more links.

http://heintz.swcollege.com

Congressional Budget Office

The CBO provides Congress with objective, timely, and nonpartisan analyses needed for economic and budget decisions, and with information and estimates needed for the Congressional budget process. Online, the CBO is a summary of Congressional activities, with updates as well as historical perspectives. The site has links to studies and reports on the Congressional budget, various documents and technical papers, as well as job opportunities.

http://www.cbo.gov/

CPA Journal

The CPA Journal online features monthly articles and outlooks, for example, "New Controls for E-Commerce." Links to monthly content and advertisers are provided.

http://www.cpajournal.com/

CPANet

This site is "the place to start..." as a resource and online community for accounting professionals. The site offers numerous links for accounting and related fields, including a Site Index, Discipline Zones (for example, accounting, assurance, audit, consulting, and more), and a Resources and Information Community (forums, newsletters, and job postings).

http://www.cpanet.com/index.asp

CPA Online

This is the "Professionsnet" website of the Australian Society of CPAs. The site contains "Professionsnet Headlines" for the world, as well as links to recruitment and careers, education and learning, and business tools.

http://www.cpaaustralia.com.au

CPA Software News

The site is designed to make software purchasing decisions easier for accounting firms. It provides a software search engine, an editorial index, a Buyer's Guide, information into trade shows, and additional links of interest.

http://www.cpasoftwarenews.com

Deloitte Touche Tohmatsu

One of the Five Big Accounting firms, Deloitte Touche Tohmatsu is dedicated to delivering "world-class accounting services" to more than 130 countries. Links on this site include those to company services--assurance and advisory, management consulting, and tax advice. In addition, there are links to global markets and careers, as well as relevant publications.

http://www.deloitte.com

Ernst and Young

This is the home page for Ernst and Young, a Big Five Accounting firm. Links on this "global business solutions" site include a career center, a library, and a "thought center." Also provided are current topics of interest in the U.S. and abroad.

http://www.ey.com

Federal Accounting Standards Advisory Board

FASAB considers and recommends accounting principles for the federal government. There are links to accounting standards and concepts, reports, news and notices, as well as meeting agenda. Another feature is the "Frequently Asked Questions" section.

http://www.fasab.gov

Financial Accounting Standards Board

The FASB is an instrument from the private sector to establish and improve standards of financial accounting and reporting for the guidance and education of the public, including issuers, auditors, and users of financial information. The site has links to technical projects, publications, and careers, as well as the feature "Understanding Issues" of the FASB.

http://www.fasb.org

Free Annual Reports

This Public Registers Annual Report Service site includes a search engine for finding annual reports, which may be obtained for free. The site includes a stock survey, corporate window, and the top 50 financial web sites.

http://www.prars.com

General Accounting Office of USA

GAO exists to oversee federal Congressional programs and operations in order to assure acountability to the American public. It is an investigative arm of Congress, and supports Congress in meeting Constitutional responsibilities. This site provides links to issues in Congressional accountability, integrity, and reliability, as well as to GAO products, publications, and employment opportunities.

http://www.gao.gov

General Services Administration of the U.S.

GSA's mission is to provide expertly managed space, supplies, services, and solutions, at the best value, to Federal employees. The site has links to public services, information, travel, transporting goods, real estate services, and others. In addition are links to GSA jobs, news releases, and Congressional testimony.

http://www.gsa.gov

Glossary of Accounting Fund Terminology

This Financial Information System Web Administrative Guide offers a glossary of both operating and non-operating funds, and provides links to Financial Services and Budget Home Page.

http://www.fis.umd.umich.edu/adguide/Glossary.htm

Government Accounting Standards Board

GASB establishes and improves standards of state and local governmental accounting and financial reporting to provide useful information for users of financial reports and to guide and educate the public. Links on this site include technical projects, performance measures, publications, and news center.

http://www.gasb.org

Institute of Chartered Accountants in England and Wales

This organization is the largest professional accountancy body in Europe. Useful links on this site include How to Become a Chartered Accountant, How to Find a Chartered Accountant, and library and other professional information, including Students and Training. The site also offers help in using the links and information provided.

http://www.icaew.co.uk

Institute of Internal Auditors

The IIA is organized to be the primary international professional association of auditors. Organized on a worldwide basis, it is dedicated to the promotion and development of internal auditing. In addition to information about the IIA itself, links on this site include news releases and publications.

http://www.theiia.org

Internal Auditing World Wide Web

This site of the IAWWW provides information and knowledge of the Internal Auditing Profession and Functions. Among the featured links are the Auditor's Bookshelf, careers, people lists, related associations, state and industry information.

http://bitwise.net/iawww

International Accounting Standards Committee

IASC is an independent private-sector group working to achieve uniformity in accounting principles for financial reporting around the world. Links provided by this site include those to the latest news of the IASC and related events, such as committee meetings and results and discussion papers.

http://www.iasc.org.uk

International Monetary Fund (IMF) Publications

This site is the Search Engine for IMF publications. Links include Working Papers in full text, as well as Country Reports, Economic Issues, and Policy Discussion Papers in full text.

http://www.imf.org/external/pubind.htm

KPMG

This home page of KPMG International, one of the Big Five Accounting firms, provides information of KPMG services--assurance, consulting, tax and legal services, among others, and offers links to its global services, global industries, as well as careers.

http://www.kpmg.com

Luca Pacioli: The Father of Accounting

This site provides an historical perspective of accounting through the biographical paper by Flyn Flesher on Luca Pacioli. In addition to the biography, the site offers further links, a bibliography, research information, and pictures.

http://members.tripod.com/~FlynF/pacioli.htm

National Association of Local Government Auditors

NALGA disseminates information and ideas about financial and performance auditing, provides training, and offers a national forum to discuss auditing issues. The site includes selections from the Local Government Auditing Quarterly and links to audit resources, audit quality, and professional information.

http://www.nalga.org

National Association of State Auditors, Comptrollers and Treasurers

This NASACT site offers information on a variety of management topics from the states' perspective. Included are a schedule of current and future events, online resources, and conferences and seminars. An additional feature is the "Washington Connection," which provides updates of federal legislative and regulatory issues.

http://www.nasact.org

National Association of State Boards of Accountancy (NASBA)

The NASBA is a forum for the nation's state boards of accountancy, which administer the Uniform CPA Examination, license certified public accountants, and regulate the practice of public accountancy in the United States. The NASBA site provides information into membership into the NASBA, licensure and practice, examinations, and professional education information.

http://www.nasba.org

Non-Profit Resource Center

This site provides accounting standards and government regulations for non-profits such as the FASB, the OMB, the AICPA, and GAO. Included on the site are a Financial Accounting Standards Menu, OMB Circulars Menu, and Other Resources Menu.

http://www.1800net.com/nprc

Pricewaterhouse Coopers

The home page of Pricewaterhouse Coopers, one of the Big Five Accounting firms, presents PwC as a part of a "global community." Available on the site is "What's New," a summary of upcoming events, as well as executive perspectives, careers, and links to current publications. Also included is information on PwC worldwide.

http://www.pwcglobal.com

QuickBooks

This commercial site offers help for small businesses in payroll tax filings and state and federal tax payments. The site offers access to professional advisors, a newsletter on small business issues, and links to QuickBook products.

http://www.quickbooks.com

Rutgers Accounting Web

RAW is the largest accounting web site on the Internet. It provides a search engine, accounting resources, the Hasselback Directory, an Accounting Research Directory, and links to accounting organizations: AAA, ACUA, AGA, FASB, GASB, IIA, IMA, and FASAB.

http://www.rutgers.edu/Accounting/

SmartPros Accounting

This site provides news, research materials, continuing education, and other essential products and services designed to aid professionals in saving time and money, and in more effectively serving clients and organizations. The site includes areas of interest, such as financial planning, and links to Member Services, Career Center, Resource Library, Professional Education, and Marketplace.

http://accounting.pro2net.com/

Tax and Accounting Sites Directory

This directory is a comprehensive index of tax, accounting, and related resources on the Internet. Some of the links provided are Tax Sites, including tax law, software, CPE, careers, and finance and investing; Accounting Sites, among them information systems, software, and accounting jobs and careers; and posted and featured Tax and Accounting Jobs.

http://www.taxsites.com

Tax Web

The Tax Web is a consumer-oriented source for federal, state and local tax-related developments. This site provides Internet-based tax materials, including calendars, forms, legislation, publishers, tax news, and tax links.

http://www.taxweb.com

10-K WIZARD

This site provides a Search Engine for SEC filings on people, companies and industries. It also offers document downloads and full text indexing and searching.

http://www.10Kwizard.com

U.S. Tax Code On-Line

This site provides access to the United States Internal Revenue Code through tables of contents and an index by section number. Full-text searching is available, and links include Tax Resources and an explanation for using the site as a tool for tax information retrieval.

http://www.fourmilab.ch/ustax/ustax.html

Virtual Accounting Library

Researched and published by Bloomsburg University students, the site is for accounting practitioners, educators, and students. It offers access to Internet accounting resources.

http://accounting.rutgers.edu/raw/resources/res.htm

ACCOUNTING FUN

Accountant Jokes

The following sites contain accountant and accounting jokes.

http://www.workjoke.com/projoke42.htm

http://www.kenbellca.com/jokes.html

http://www.jokesnjokes.net/funny.jokes.amusing.humor.laughs/Profession/accountant001.htm

Spreadsheet Jokes

The site offers "cellular humor" and asks for new submissions. It provides links to numerous jokes, among which is a "Spreadsheet Glossary" of humorous definitions pertaining to spreadsheets.

http://www.j-walk.com/ss/jokes/index.htm

Accounting Careers

Accounting.com

The Accounting.com site is designed to be an accounting and finance resource for both job seekers and employers in the profession. There is access to Job Seekers, which contains links to available jobs and a place to post resumes, and Employers, who may post jobs and search the site's Resume Database. In addition, the site provides a CPA directory, headline financial news, CPE resources, and a discussion group.

http://www.accounting.com

Careers in Accounting.com

Internet information contained in this site includes public accounting, tax, auditing, and managerial accounting. Links are provided to accounting careers and other career sites, as well as recommended books in the field.

http://www.careers-in-accounting.com

Childs, Smith & Associates

Childs, Smith & Associates is a search firm specializing in the placement of permanent and temporary accounting, audit, tax, and consulting service professionals. The purpose of the site is to match the right individual to the right career opportunity, in an effort to improve employee retention. Links include those to candidate and employer information and interview tips, as well as "Hot Tips" and "Submit Jobs" links.

http://www.accounting-jobs.com/ (See also http://www.accountingjobs.com)

Financial, Accounting, and Insurance Jobs Page

The page offers a view of available jobs in finance, accounting, and insurance, and provides a job search and job postings. The site has links to Job Seeker Resources and Featured Employers, as well as a provision for e-mailing resumes to employers.

http://www.nationjob.com/financial

Paul Clikeman

This site, a link from the home page of Accounting Professor Paul Clikeman (University of Richmond), contains links to career and other accounting sites. Included on the site are Accounting Links, Accounting News, directories of Public Accounting Firms, and more.

http://www.urich.edu/~pclikema/LINKS.HTM

CAREERS

Abbott, Langer & Associates

This site offers salary and benefits reports in a range of industries.

http://www.abbott-langer.com

America's Job Bank

This site is a partnership between the U.S. Department of Labor and the state-operated public employment service. It is for those "looking for a dream job," and offers the job seeker access to state job databases and the opportunity to create and post resumes online. Additional links for employers include resume databases and job postings.

http://www.ajb.dni.us

Ask the Headhunter

At this site, Nick Corcodilos, a headhunter and management consultant, has answered over 15,000 questions about job hunting and hiring. He is the author of Ask the Headhunter: Reinventing the Interview to Win the Job.

http://www.asktheheadhunter.com

THE BLACK COLLEGIAN

This site allows African-American job seekers the opportunity to look for jobs, create and post resumes, and establish a search agent online. The site provides "channels" to other career-related sites, including graduate and professional schools, national and international sites, and career advice. Links for employers include recruiting and managing candidates.

http://www.black-collegian.com/jobs/jobsearch.shtml

BrassRing.com

This site provides job seekers the opportunity to post resumes and search for jobs, as well as get career advice and sign up for the site's newsletter. There are also listings for career events, and links to both national and international sites.

http://www.brassring.com

CareerBuilder

This "mega job search" site offers featured jobs and links to job search tools such as salaries and counseling. In addition, the page has a "My Career Builder" feature which enables job seekers to post resumes and obtain a personal search agent, and more.

http://www.careerbuilder.com

Career.com

This recruitment page provides an opportunity to search for jobs and post resumes. It includes an employer menu, ad rates, and other resources, as well as links to "Hot Jobs" and a "CyberFair."

http://www.career.com

Career Development eManual

This site, by the career development department at the University of Waterloo's (Canada), provides career development activities.

http://www.cdm.uwaterloo.ca

Career Key

This site is an online career networking resource whose purpose is to provide an awareness of the career marketplace and access to the "hidden job market." The page offers valuable tools for the job hunter, including "Career Search," "Career Resources," such as resume resources, interviewing, salary surveys, and research aids, and a comprehensive directory of "Industry Links." Included in the site is also a featured "Career Article of the Month," and recent job postings in the United States and Canada.

http://www.careerkey.com

CareerMagazine

The site offers a "Feature of the Week" section, which provides information on current happenings in the job market, and "Today's Hot Topics." Links include those to job searches, employers, miscellaneous articles, a message board, and products and services.

http://www.careermag.com

Career Resource Center

Among the sites available from this directory site are headhunter.net, USJobBoard.com, JobBankUSA, ResumeZapper.com and others. Links include "Jobs Now," employers, career services, and career references.

http://www.careers.org

CareerSite.com

For job candidates, this site has access to 25,000+ employers. The job seeker has the oportunity to find jobs, post a resume, and do an employer search. Employers are provided the tools to build recruitment sites.

http://www.careersite.com

CNET TechJobs

This job search site includes links to numerous job listings. Also included are tips on resume writing and professional downloads.

http://coverage.cnet.com/techjobs/0-7067.html

Employment Guide's Career Web

This site provides links to a Jobseeker Center, an Employer Center, and affiliate sites. Links include featured jobs and employers, as well as tools for job searching, and for posting resumes and jobs.

http://www.cweb.com

FedWorld U.S. Government Federal Job Search

This FJOB site includes a National Technical and Information Service, and International Trade and Business Store. Links go to a database which allows the job seeker to search abstracts of open federal government jobs. Listed are summer jobs, and jobs by state and region.

http://www.fedworld.gov/jobs/jobsearch.html

HotJobs.com

This site is a Yahoo! company, offering job seekers tools and advice. HotJobs provides employers and staffing agencies with progressive recruiting solutions and hiring management software.

http://www.hotjobs.com

I-Resign

Among the offerings of this site are a free template for resignation letters and information on how to resign a current job, including a Complete Guide to Resigning, and a Guide to Resigning with Style and Dignity. There is much more to the site, however, including resources such as Job Hunting, with advice and insight into finding the next job, and a General Discussion forum. The page offers featured articles and opinions, as well as articles on CVs, cover letters, and interviews. In addition, there are links to such financial tools as US Federal Tax Estimator and Salary Calculator.

http://www.i-resign.com

JobHuntersBible.com

Dick Bolles is the guide to this JobHuntersBible Web site. The site is designed as a supplement to his book, What Color Is Your Parachute? The page is divided into two sections, the "Net Guide," which includes a job search and creating and posting resumes, and a "Parachute Library" of related publications.

http://www.jobhuntersbible.com

jobs.com

This site for job seekers provides a job search tool, the opportunity to create and post resumes, and links to related communities. In addition are links to resources, and a "Get Started" feature which show the seeker how to find a job in "three easy steps."

http://www.jobs.com

JOBTRAK.COM

This is the home page for Monster TRAK.com. It is a site for students and offers links to job searches, college staff, and other resources. Among the job search tools are an employer's showcase, a career guide, a "major to career converter," and a virtual interview.

http://www.jobtrak.com

Monster Job Board

The site provides over 1,000,000 job postings. It offers a Career Center, in which the job seeker can search 3000 pages of career advice, resume help, and interview tips. Elements of the site are its "Featured Employers" and a global network directory.

http://www.monster.com

National Association of Colleges and Employers JobWeb

This site provides an employer search, which researches the organization before the interview, and a JobWeb data base for obtaining more information on organizations that hire college graduates. There are also links to an online career fair and tools for impressing prospective employers.

http://www.jobweb.org

Occupational Outlook Handbook [Bureau of Labor Statistics]

This is the government web site for the current Occupational Outlook Handbook. The site has directions for finding career information: search tips, an A-Z index, and cluster buttons leading to various occupations.

http://www.bls.gov/oco

Wall Street Journal

This is the site for the WSJ.com Career Journal. Links include those to salary and hiring information, job hunting advice, tips on managing a career, a bookstore, and more. Other sections are "Today's Features," which is current information and news about getting jobs, and a calendar of career events.

http://careers.wsj.com

WetFeet.com

This site is designed to provide aid in making smarter career decisions. It offers links to such resources as "Career Research," including interviews, career and industry profiles, insider guides, and salary picks. There is also a "Manage Your Career" section, with links to continuing education, resume help, and more. And there is "Find a Job," with job and internship listings, as well as international listings. In addition, there are a search tool for finding a job, a featured company which may be researched, and "Career News," providing links to featured articles and expert advice. A special feature is the "Popular Insider Guide" to careers and industries.

http://www.wetfeet.com

APPENDIX

INFOTRAC
COLLEGE EDITION

InfoTrac® OneFile Plus Navigation Guide

InfoTrac® OneFile Plus Navigation Guide

InfoTrac® OneFile is a single electronic resource that provides instant access to the most current periodical and news content. Updated daily, **InfoTrac® OneFile** contains more than 26 million articles from a variety of mainstream and specialized sources – from the New York Times to refereed academic journals. With its multiple pathways to key information **InfoTrac® OneFile** is the ideal resource for anyone wanting to browse the latest news, review a set of subject areas, select a particular resource, or search across the entire database.

Sources

- Newswires – wire services covering agriculture, general news, broadcast news, government, business press releases, industry topics, sports and current events from all over the world.
- Newsletters from various specialties and business sectors
- Newspapers with full indexing of
    - The New York Times
    - The Wall Street Journal
    - The Washington Post
    - Los Angeles Times
    - Christian Science Monitor
- Periodicals (8,000 total/4,409 full-text/2,884 titles with images)
    - General interest magazines
    - Refereed academic journals
    - Business publications
    - Technology periodicals
    - Law journals
    - Health care periodicals

Search Options

InfoTrac® OneFile offers an intuitive interface that provides multiple pathways to key information. With its time-tested functionality, this essential resource is versatile and easy to use, whether you need access to the latest news, want to review a set of subject areas, select a particular publication, or search across the entire database.

There are 4 different search modes in the **InfoTrac®** interface. You can search for articles by subject or keyword. For those who want to do a "power search", an **advanced** search option is available. The advanced search can be as simple or as complex as you would like. **Relevance** search is also available and performs a search that is similar to search engines on the web. The results list from a relevance search will display those articles that most closely match your topic first.

Main Search Screen

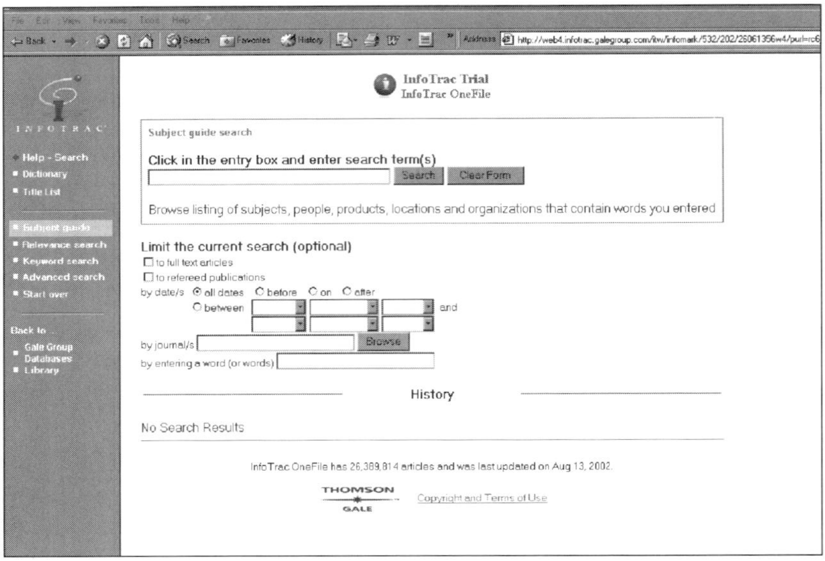

Most often Subject search is the default search. If it is not, click on the link Subject Guide in the navigation bar (blue area on the left-hand side of the screen.) This will allow you to search your topic by subject headings. If InfoTrac does not find the subject terms you entered, it will default to a keyword search. If a keyword result is not found, then the database assumes the term was misspelled and gives you a list of similar terms. You can click on the appropriate word to link to the subject heading.

Subject headings are assigned by a group of indexers at Gale using our own controlled vocabulary, which is based on Library of Congress Subject Headings. Because of this indexing subject search typically returns the most on-target search results. It is most useful for single topic searches.

You can limit your subject search (or any search) before you enter it or after you receive results. See the section on Limiting Options for more information.

Subject Search

1. Click in the search box and type the word **astronomy**. Press Enter or click the **Search** button to start the search.

2. The subject guide list will be displayed on the screen. Every subject heading with the word **astronomy** is listed in alphabetical order where **astronomy** is the first word, then where **astronomy** is the second word, then where astronomy is the third word, and etc. *Notice the "See" and "See also" references; this is one of the strengths of a controlled vocabulary. If you were to do a keyword search on the word "china," you would find articles on the country and the porcelain. Subject search uses controlled vocabulary to find only articles that match your exact topic.*

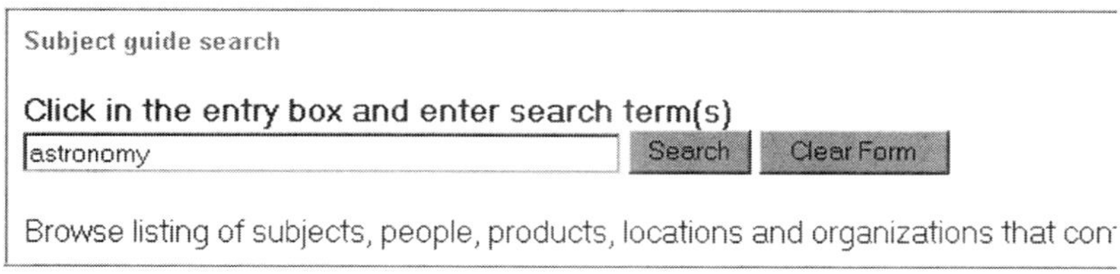

From the subject guide list you can click to view articles by source type (newspapers or periodicals). Often, you can narrow periodical articles by subdivision. This is an example of how precise subject searching can be.

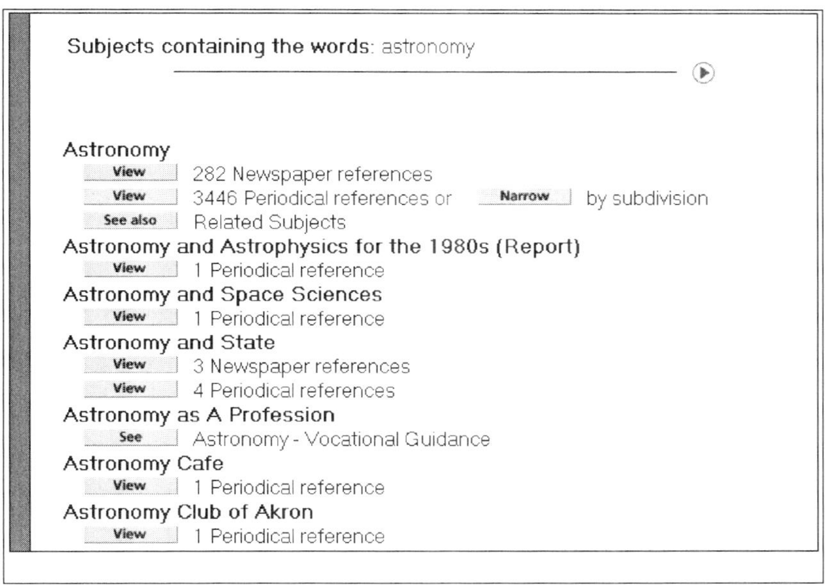

3. Click on the word "Narrow" to view a list of subjects from which to choose.

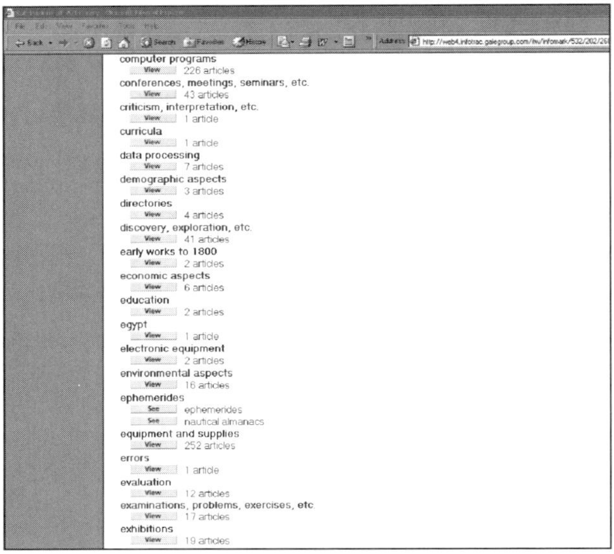

4. View the articles listed under the subdivision **discover, exploration, etc,** This will take you to your Citation List.

<u>Citation List (Results List)</u>

The articles on a citation list are sorted in reverse chronological order. The only exception is relevance search – those results are sorted in relevance order.

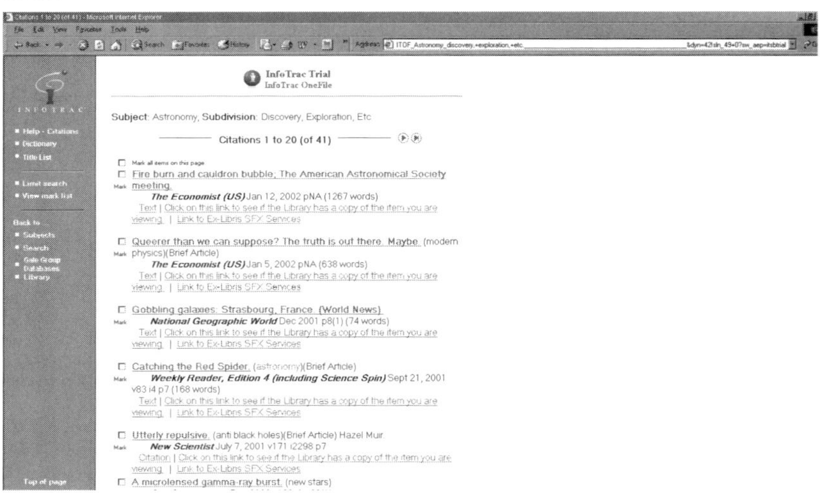

Your citation list always shows your search strategy at the top of the page. There are twenty citations per page; you have next page, previous page, first page and last page icons at the top and bottom of the citation list page. There is a Limit Search button on the navigation bar that will allow you to narrow your results by full text, refereed, date, journal name, and keyword if needed.

The citations give a brief description of the article. From the citation you can tell what information the database contains for the article: **citation** – a citation and indexing that describes the article; **abstract** – a citation, indexing, and a brief summary of the article; **text** – full text of the article; **text with graphics** – full text of the articles with images from the article. This information is shown as a link directly beneath the citation.

The title of the article is a hyperlink; you may click it or the citation, abstract, text, text with graphics link to view the article.

Mark List

You may also save documents in a Mark List for reading in more detail later. Simply check the box next to the title in the Results List. The documents you checked will be put in a Mark List and a new button will appear on the left side of the screen labeled "View Mark List." From within an article, you can check the box next to the article to also add it to the Mark List automatically as well.

Article View

Article view has several features that allow you to work with your article.

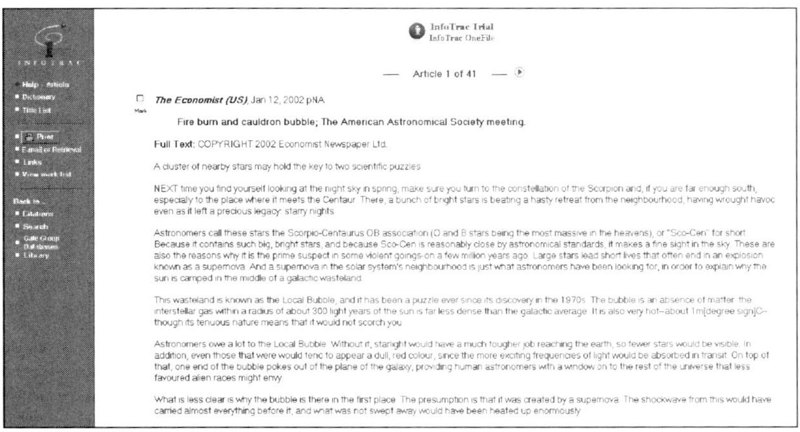

Using the arrows that appear at the top and bottom of screen allows you to move between articles on your results list.

The citation for your article appears at the top of the page.
Printing and e-mailing options appear at the bottom of the article. You may also be able to download the article in PDF format and see it in it's original format (using Adobe Acrobat Reader.)

The subject headings that have been assigned to the article appear below. These headings are linked to other articles on the same topic. All users, including those using ADA devices for the visually impaired, can click on these links to see "more like this."

Back To Section

The Back To Section on your navigation bar allows you to jump back to a previous point in the database. It allows you to do with one click what would take several clicks on the Back button on your browser. Your Back To options will change as you move around in the database.

Keyword Search

Click on the link **Keyword Search** in the navigation bar. This will allow you to search your topic by keywords. You have the option of searching for your topic in the title, citation, and abstract or in the entire article content (full text.) A Keyword Search looks for the word or words entered. Results are listed from most recent to oldest publication date.

Keyword search comes in most handy when trying to answer reference questions. Whereas with subject search, you may only enter one topic at a time, you can search on several topics in keyword search.

Click in the search box and type the words **olympic gold medal!** (the exclamation mark is used as a wildcard; this will find medal or medals; for more on wildcards please refer to the section on Wildcards.) Choose to search in **search in title, citation, abstract.** Click on **Search** button to start the search.

Remember, keyword search only searches for your search terms entered; unlike subject search where you can find see and see also references to refer you to the right topic.

Relevance Search

A Relevance Search is similar to keyword search in that it bypasses the subject index and looks for your terms to appear in an article. The main difference between the two is that relevance search results will sort according to their relevance to the search terms. This is determined by where the words appear in the article (title, text, etc.) and how closely they match the original search terms (exact match, word variant, etc.)

Relevance search does four main things differently than all the other search paths:

1. Sorts results in relevance order.
2. Uses implied truncation – wildcards are not needed or accepted.
3. Will not return more than 200 hits.
4. Disregards logical and Boolean operators. AND, OR, NOT will not work as operators at relevance search – they are read as search terms.

To find exact words/phrases:

Enclose searches that are for exact words or phrase with quotation marks ("...").

e.g. "Internet service provider"

Inclusion of specific terms:

Because Boolean operators are ignored at relevance search you must use another way to force the search engine to find all your terms. Place a plus sign (+) before a term or terms to ensure that InfoTrac does search for that part of the word or phrase. Any results that do not include the term or terms with a plus sign before it will be rejected. *Using plus signs may not be needed because all of your search terms are searched for initially; the database will only resort to searching for less if not enough articles are found.*

e.g. +drilling +contractors

InfoTrac will look for only articles that have the word contractors in them and also include the word drilling. Any articles with just the word drilling without the word contractors will not appear in the results list.

Exclusion of specific terms:

Because Boolean operators are ignored at relevance search you must use another way to exclude terms from your search results. Place a minus sign before a term or terms to ensure that InfoTrac does NOT search for that part of the word or phrase.

e.g. –Cuban jazz

InfoTrac will search for articles with the word jazz in them but will not include any articles that also include the word Cuban in the results list.

Click on the **Relevance Search** link in the navigation bar. The articles that are considered to be most relevant to your search terms will be listed first.

Relevance Search Example: To highlight the differences between Keyword Search and Relevance Search let's try our **olympic gold medal** search again. Remember we won't need to use the exclamation point as a wildcard; relevance search uses implied truncation.

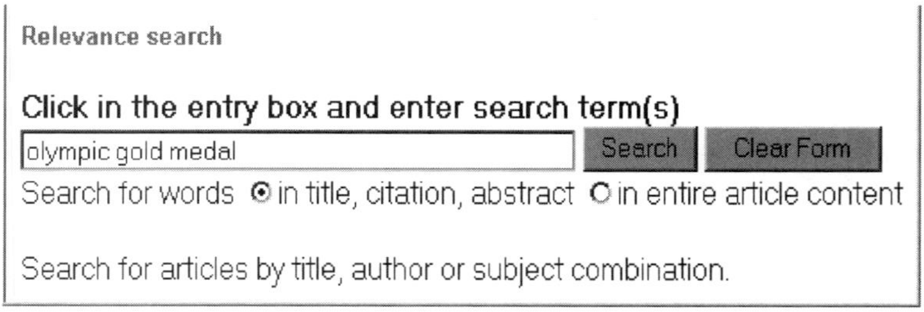

In your citation page, articles are ranked by percentages, not dates, and listed in order from the highest percentile to the lowest within a cap of the top 200 most relevant articles. Our keyword search results sorted in reverse chronological order so we got very recent articles

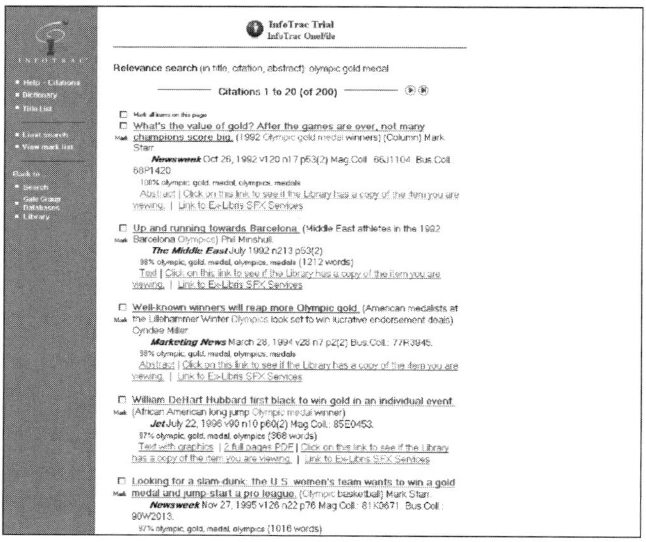

listed first. The relevance search results sorted by relevance so our first page of hits may be a little more on target. Keyword search looks for your terms to appear in the article but doesn't consider if the article is really about that subject. Relevance search looks for your terms in the article and sorts the results by how often the search term is mentioned in relation to the length of the article. You'll find fewer "false hits" with a relevance search. If date is important to your relevance search you can always limit your search by date.

Advanced Search

The Advanced Search provides searchers with the most control because you choose the fields that it searches.

Advanced Search lets you create complex search expressions. A search expression is composed of any of one or more index abbreviations, your search term and search operators (if needed.) A search expression might also contain one or more result sets from the History list, designated *R1*, *R2*, and so on. **Hint**: It's often best to perform compound searches one step at a time and then to combine the result sets. This assures you that each part of the search is working.

INDEXES

In most cases, even if the indexes below are not shown in your Select an Index box, they may still be used.

Index	Abbr.	Content
Abstract	ab	Words in abstracts and authors' abstracts
Author	au	Names of article authors
Content	ac	"fulltext," "image," or "abstract"
Date	da	Publication dates of articles
ISSN	is	International Standard Serial Number
Issue Number	iu	Issue number of the publication you are searching
Journal Name	jn	Specify publications in this database
Keyword	ke	Words in titles, title annotations, authors, abstracts and assigned index terms
Record Number	rn	One per article
Start page	sp	Starting page number of the article you wish to find
Subject	su	Words from indexed subject headings
Subject List	su=	Browse list of subject headings
Text Word	tx	Words in article text
Title	ti	Words in article title
Vol. Number	vo	Volume number of the publication you are searching.

For some of the operators listed above you may use the limiting options instead. For example, the limit by date option can be used instead of the date index (da).

HOW TO PERFORM AN ADVANCED SEARCH
If your advanced search screen looks like this use Option 1.

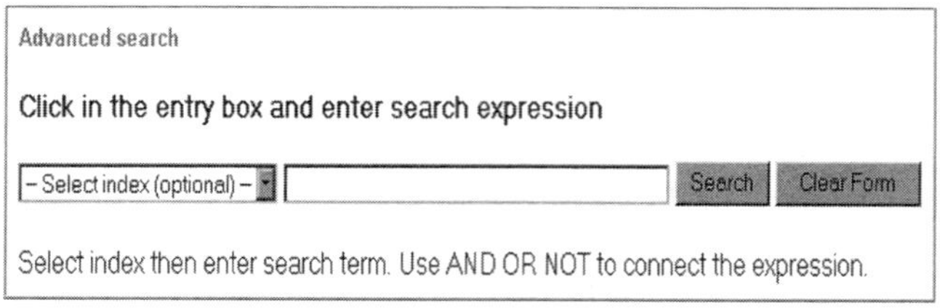

Option 1: Searching in Advanced Search involves four steps:
1. Choose an index by selecting it from the **Select Index** drop box.
2. Click on the entry box (after the index abbreviation).
3. Enter one or more words, using wildcards if desired.
4. Click on **Search**.
5. Select your results from the **History** list.

Step 1 is optional. If you don't choose an index, the keyword index is searched. You could also type in the index abbreviation.

To combine indexes you can use logical and other search operators (see below for explanation) in your search expression (e.g., jobs or employment), except when you are browsing.

If your advanced search screen looks like this use Option 2.

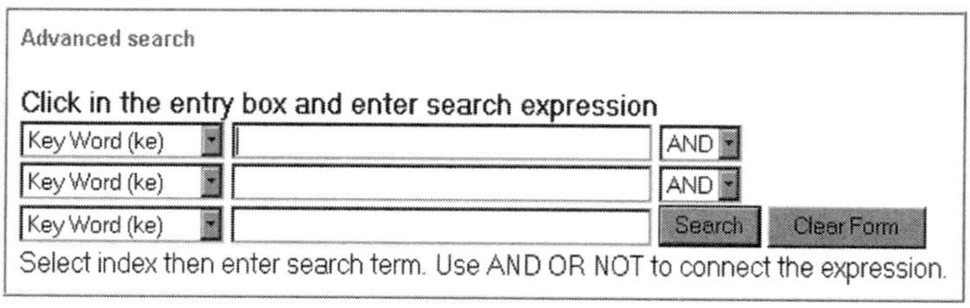

Option 2: This format is like filling out a search form:
1. Choose your index from the drop box.
2. Enter the appropriate search term in the box across from the index.
3. Click Search.
4. You may need to view your results by choosing them from your history list.

Click on the **Advanced Search** link in the navigation bar. Advanced Search can be as simple or as complex as you need. Let's try and find an article written by humorist Dave Barry; the title is *Final Judgment on the Salt Lake City Winter Games*, published in February 2002.

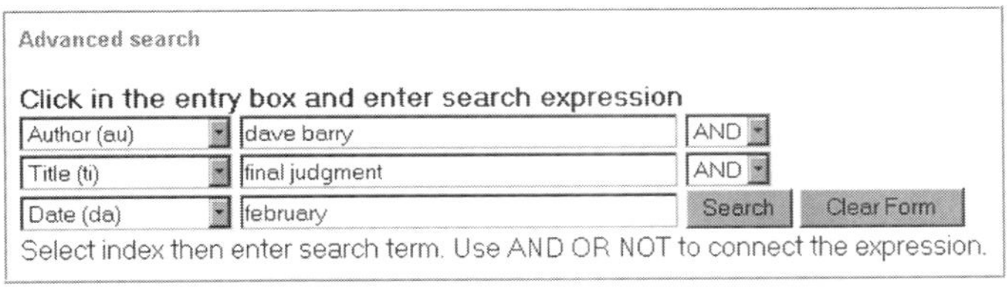

By using the Author Index we're sure to find articles written by Dave Barry, not about him. When using the title index you can search on the entire article title or any portion of it. Instead of using the Date Index we could have used the Date limit option – they are interchangeable.

To view your results you may need to choose the correct result from your history list.

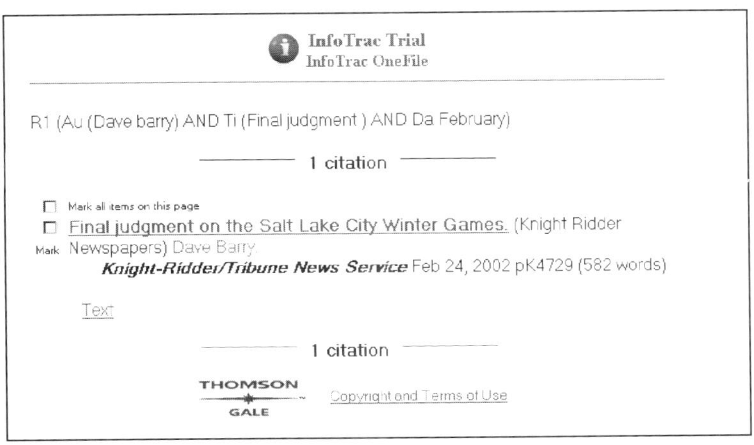

SFX

InfoTrac Web has been enhanced to function as an SFX "source" – meaning it is capable of sending outbound requests to an SFX server. This upgrade to the InfoTrac Web product line supports the open linking environment of the SFX OpenURL Framework. SFX is a context sensitive, electronic resource installed and configured to run on a library computer. Libraries must purchase the software through Ex-Libris.

The most significant advantage of SFX is that it facilitates linking between citations and full text, even when different vendors host the citation and full text data. SFX can also be used to facilitate context sensitive searching across "targeted" library resources, as long as the resource supports the OpenURL standard. The OpenURL standard is the framework that SFX services operate on.

An "SFX" icon appears at the end of a citation in the result list. By clicking on the SFX icon, InfoTrac will send an "outbound" request, in the form of an OpenURL, to an SFX server.

For example, the article below in **InfoTrac® OneFile** from *The New York Times* is a citation; you can use the SFX link to find the full text:

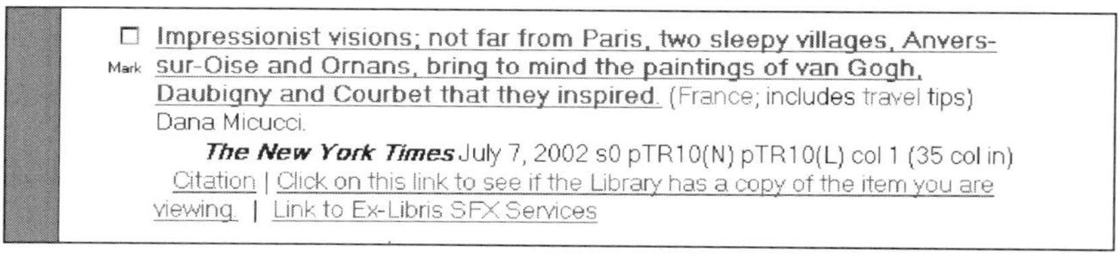

When the SFX button is clicked, SFX selected and configured resources display in an SFX window. From the SFX window, click on the SFX resource of your choice and SFX works to link or retrieve results from that resource.

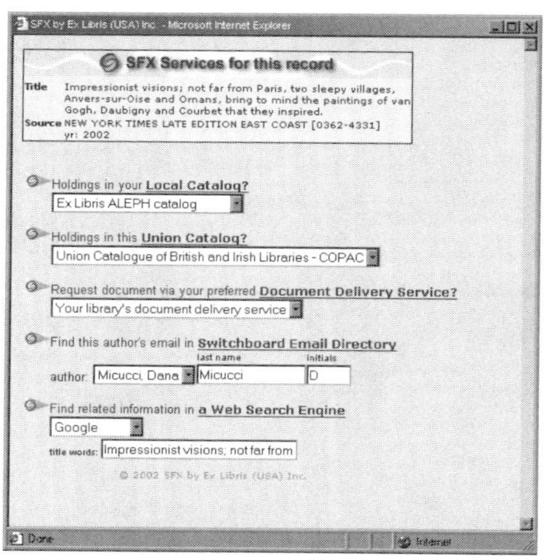

A new window opens and the result of the SFX request is available. InfoTrac Web subscribers can enable SFX support for their products through the Location and Preference setting modules using their InfoTrac Config account. For setup information, an SFX Technical Bulletin is available from the Gale Group Web site at: www.galegroup.com or from our Customer Resource Center Technical Support staff.

Limiting Options

You can limit a search result by using the options that appear at the bottom of each search page. The limit options are also available from the citation list by clicking the limit search button. The limit options you may have available to you are:

To articles with full text

Limits your search to articles with text or text with graphics. Place a check in this box by clicking on it.

To articles from refereed (peer-reviewed) publications

Refereed journals are those in which articles, before they are published, must be reviewed by a body of peers, experts in the same field as the writer. Peer review does not guarantee that an article is correct, but it does help ensure that data and methodology have met a high standard. Articles from non-refereed journals might also meet the same standards, but no committee has certified that this is so. You can limit the results of your search to include only articles from refereed journals. Click on the box to impose or remove this limitation.

By date

You can limit a search result to include only material published on, before or after a date or within a range of dates. Use the radio buttons to choose how you want to limit by date, then use the drop-down boxes to select the exact date or dates that you want. If your date limit option is an empty search field you may use several different formats for limiting:

3/28/2001	1998-2000	2002	<1995	Jan 2001 – June 2002
March 28 2001	1998 to 2000	March 1998	>1998	1/2001 – 6/2002

To articles from the following journals (publications)

You can limit a search in one of two ways. You can search journal (publication) names containing certain words. Or, you can search only articles from as many as ten journals (publications) selected from a list.

To limit your search to journals with names containing specific words, just click on the **by journal** entry box, and type one or more words. Because the search is matching words in journal names, there's a potential for unintended matches even if you enter the entire name. For example, the search **new york** would match not only *New York* magazine but also *The New York Times* and *The New York Times Magazine*. To get only an exact match, enclose the search term in double quotes; for example, **"new york"** to match only *New York* magazine.

To limit a search to as many as ten specific journals, press the **Browse button** to see a list of publications in the currently selected collection. Once you've made your selection, the box will contain an indication of how many publications you've chosen. Click on the arrows to the right of the box if you want to choose a single publication from your list for any given search. Then, press the **Search button** to execute your request.

To entries containing the word(s)
You can limit a search result by adding one or more words to the current search that must be found in matching articles. You can leave in words such as the and a even though these are stop words and are not indexed. You can use wildcards, logical operators and nesting operators. This option actually performs a keyword search in the title, citation, and abstract fields. It comes in most handy when you'd like to combine a subject search with a keyword search.

General Search Strategies

- InfoTrac searches for your words within two words of each other in either direction (to allow for variations).
- The more search terms you add, the more precise your search results will be.

  e.g. computer (results=1,450,945)
  computer programming (results=5,444)
  computer programming language (results=293)
- Be specific. Enter all those terms in your search rather than just one word.

Stop Words

Stop words are small words that are not indexed. Stop words include such words as a, and, etc., in, of, on and to; the actual list varies depending on how you're searching. The system recognizes stop words and knows how to search as if they weren't there.

Wildcards

Sometimes you might want to find more than just exact matches to a search term. *Wildcards* let you substitute symbols for one or more letters. With wildcards, you can match

- both the singular and plural forms of a word
- words that begin with the same root
- words that can be spelled in different ways

You can even match words that you're not sure how to spell!

There are three wildcard operators:

- An **asterisk** (*) stands for **any number of characters**, including none, and is especially useful when you want to find all words that share the same root. For example, **pigment*** matches *pigment, pigments, pigmentation*, etc. An asterisk can also be used within a word, but the other wildcards are more precise for this kind of use.

- A **question mark** (?) stands for **exactly one character** and is especially useful when you're uncertain of a spelling. For example, a search like **relev?nce** means you can match the word relevance even if, like many of us, you can't remember whether it's spelled with ance or ence.

  A question mark is also useful for finding certain words with variant spellings. For example, **defen?e** finds both *defense* (American) and *defence* (British and Canadian). Multiple question marks in a row stand for the same number of characters as there are question marks. For example, **psych????y** matches either *psychology* or *psychiatry* but not *psychotherapy*.

- An **exclamation point** (!) stands for **one or no characters** and is especially useful when you want to match the singular and plural of a word but not other forms. For example, **product!** matches *product* and *products* but not *productive* or *productivity*. The exclamation point can also be used inside a word to match certain variant spellings. For example, **colo!r** matches both *color* (American) and *colour* (British).

If you see a message about a search being invalid, you'll need to add at least one character before one of the wildcards.

Exact Words/Phrases:

Enclose searches that are for exact words or a phrase with quotation marks ("...").

e.g. "Internet service provider"

Nesting Operators

You can change the evaluation order of the logical operators by using nesting operators (parentheses). When you nest entries, the search system performs the operation within parentheses first, then merges the result with the part of the entry outside the parentheses.

- The search expression **race or color and discrimination** specifies that you want to find records that contain either the word race or both the words *color* and *discrimination*. This expression is equivalent to the expression **race or (color and discrimination)**.
- The search expression **(race or color) and discrimination** specifies that you want to find records that contain either or both of the words *race* or *color* and that also contain the word *discrimination*.

Logical Operators

- AND—The **and** operator specifies that both words on either side of the operator must occur in the part of a record you're searching for that record to match. For example, **alcohol and pregnancy** finds only those records in which both the word *alcohol* and the word *pregnancy* occur.

- OR— The **or** operator specifies that one or the other or both of the words on either side of the operator must occur in the part of a record you're searching for that record to match. For example, **dreams or daydreams** finds records in which either the word *dreams* or the word *daydreams* or both occur.

- NOT— The **not** operator specifies that the word before the operator must occur but the word after the operator must not occur for a record to match. For example, **crime not murder** finds all records in which the word *crime* occurs *except* the ones in which the word *murder* also occurs.

Logical operators in a search expression are evaluated in a particular order:
1. not and and
2. or

If you want to change the order of evaluation, use the nesting operators.

Proximity Operators

- **The W operator**—finds essays containing the specified words in the specific order within the number of words you indicate

  e.g. Peking w2 opera

  This search will find the word Peking within 2 words of opera, but opera must follow Peking.
- **The N operator**—locates essays containing the words you specify within the number of words you indicate, but the words can be in ANY order

  e.g. electronic n2 book.

  The search will find the word "electronic" within 2 words of "book" in any direction.

InfoMarks

An InfoMark at the top of any page indicates that the URL of the page persists even when the session is over. Persistent URLs can be book marked for future reference or copied into an electronic mail message or onto a Web page. InfoMarks lets you save and re-launch searches and embed them on Web pages, e-mail, word processing documents, and more. With a click of the mouse, you can access a comprehensive knowledge base that you have designed. InfoMarks is the premier tool for creating reading lists, course packs, study guides, content services, guidelines for special projects, bibliographies, training sites, electronic journal directories, and so much more. You could track an author InfoMark the search, then revisit the new and updated data as often as you like.

For more information on how to use InfoMarks, click the icon from within OneFile or refer to the website www.galegroup.com/infomarks.

For more information about these tips and additional information about **InfoTrac® OneFile, check out the Help feature located in the margin on the left-hand side of each screen.